ESSENTIALS OF EIGHTEENTH-CENTURY COUNTERPOINT

ESSENTIALS OF EIGHTEENTH-CENTURY COUNTERPOINT

A Practical Stylistic Approach

Neale B. Mason

Associate Professor, Department of Music
Murray State University, Murray, Kentucky

WM. C. BROWN COMPANY PUBLISHERS
Dubuque, Iowa

Copyright © 1968 by
Wm. C. Brown Company Publishers

Library of Congress Catalog Card Number: 67–21314

ISBN 0–697–03605–7

Third Printing, 1970

Printed in the United States of America

Preface

"What good is counterpoint going to do us?" "Why do we have to study this stuff?" Questions such as these are hurled at most counterpoint teachers every year by disgruntled undergraduates who never considered music to consist of anything more than jam sessions and band and choir tours.

Often we try to brush aside the questioners with remarks about overcoming "musical illiteracy" or such. Perhaps, instead, we should ask ourselves these questions, and try to come up with plausible answers. The obvious sometimes becomes difficult to explain when subjected to close scrutiny. Too many schools are seeing fit to eliminate courses in counterpoint, or to pare them down, or to make them elective. It would seem that many administrations have not been able to find an answer that would stand up before the onslaught of added requirements in science, the liberal arts, and professional education.

If we are going to answer these questions — which we *must* do — then we need to begin with the premise that the musician is a professional, whether he be a composer, a performer, or a teacher. The basic training of a professional must be as complete as possible in order that he may acquire the information and the skills needed to cope with the materials and problems of his profession efficiently and knowledgeably. The study of counterpoint is one of the more important of these "background" courses. Since the practice of counterpoint, or at least the use of contrapuntal techniques, forms a vital and generous part of much of the music of our heritage, and is inherent in the best of contemporary music as well, then it would seem obvious that acquiring at least an intellectual, if not indeed a practical, command of this technique should be an integral part of the training of a musician if he is to be worthy of his professional status.

Ideally, no one should draw conclusions on the basis of a small segment of any single period, or on the output of any individual composer.

J. S. Bach is more than an individual composer. He is a whole era in himself. In his music is combined the Germanic scholasticism as his natural heritage, along with the Latin vitality acquired from his admiration for and avid study of his Italian contemporaries and immediate predecessors. It is hard to conceive that a Mozart, a Beethoven, a Mendelssohn, or a Brahms, a Franck, a Reger, or even a Hindemith could have arisen without a Bach to precede him.

The counterpoint students who asked the earlier questions could well have that right if they were being subjected to a study of counterpoint in the manner of the stilted, unnatural texts which appeared at the beginning of the century. In these texts, the Cantus Firmus reared its frowning head over row on row of meaningless rules, and never should the element of living music be allowed to intrude! (Or, at least, only that small part which seemed to conform briefly with the imaginative restrictions of the author.)

Faced with such a situation, it is no wonder that students, and often teachers as well, threw up their hands and relegated the whole subject of counterpoint to the junk pile, or withdrew into the safe, comfortable field of sixteenth-century counterpoint, where rules had meaning in music.

This text has evolved, as many do, not from the desire to write a textbook (who, in his right mind, would do this?) but to find a more interesting, more efficient approach to my own teaching problems. Through class after class, and revision after revision, the exercises evolved, and the presentation clarified itself, as I tried to satisfy my students' questions and anticipate their problems, until the results began to balance out the effort.

One of the most difficult points to deliver is that of style. With this problem in mind, exercises were developed, along the lines of good harmony exercises, which would help the student to become familiar, through association, with the characteristics he would find in the actual music.

Analysis of the music of Bach is of extreme importance in bringing together the small details and demonstrating their practical use and relationship, as well as in the valuable experience of exposing the student to this music as much as possible.

The value of writing an invention or a fugue is often questioned, with the argument that "we aren't going to be composers," but the assignments in writing are intended to be reasonable continuations of the working-out of the exercises and the application of discoveries made in analysis, not to develop composers as such, but to bring forth the realization that this is real, live music which was written by real, live composers. I have seen many an average student suddenly blossom forth as the realization is reached that he can write, and it can sound. From this experience he may not become a composer, for this takes a special flair, but through this he becomes a more confident, a more professional, musician.

It is with humility that I offer this text to my fellow teachers of counterpoint. We have common problems which I have solved, at least, for myself. If this presentation is of aid to others, then "my cup runneth over."

My most grateful appreciation for the aid and encouragement I have received in the evolution and preparation of this text is extended to Dr. Frederick W. Westphal, Music Editor, Wm. C. Brown Company; to Prof. Robert Kelly, University of Illinois, to the Committee on Institutional Studies and Research, Murray State University, and, most of all, to my wife, Dorothy.

—*Neale B. Mason*

Introduction

The study of Counterpoint is a stylistic one, whether it be the "strict" counterpoint of the sixteenth century or the "free" counterpoint of the seventeenth and eighteenth centuries. This means that, in order to have validity, it must be a study of the practices of the composers of the period through close examination of the music itself. From this comes understanding, respect, and a development of musical values which all take their place in the development of that nebulous characteristic called "musicianship." This is the reason we turn to Bach, the greatest of the contrapuntal masters, for the development of a musical understanding of contrapuntal techniques.

The most available of Bach's music is his music for the keyboard, and among these works, his two-voice Inventions, Sinfonias, and the Fugues of the *Well-Tempered Clavier* seem to contain his testament of beliefs as completely as any small body of works can. This is the reason that these works are chosen for source material in this text. There are other works equally as revealing, notably the organ Fugues and the Chorale Preludes, but none is as concise or as easily approachable as the works chosen.

It is recommended, therefore, that the student be supplied with copies of these works:

> *The Two- and Three-Part Inventions* (*Sinfonias*)
> *The Well-Tempered Clavier,* Book I

In addition, it is helpful to have available:

> *The Well-Tempered Clavier,* Book II
> *The Goldberg Variations*

No special edition is required, although those with analysis of form already appearing should be avoided. The Kalmus editions are clear, uncluttered, and easy to use, as are certain others. It should be noted that overedited versions, with written-out trills and ornaments, can tend to be confusing. The Lea Pocket scores, reproductions of the *Bachgesellschaft,* are authoritative and, while in small print, are an excellent source.

As in a course in harmony, the technical problems need to be understood before the musical events can be appreciated. It is to this end that written exercises have been conceived that will develop not only a technique of writing, but a familiarity with the style to be encountered in the study of the actual music.

Sterile, often unfounded, rules and restrictions have been avoided as much as possible, and principles and practices are substituted. This is intended to release the student from hidebound rules that frequently the composer never observes, replacing them with controls based on the music with which the student will be dealing in study and analysis.

At the end of each chapter, a group of study questions has been included, which are designed to aid the student in assimilating the materials of the chapter.

There is more material included in this text than can be used in a normal one-year course of study. This allows the teacher to make selective choices for his course content. In Part I, the main stress should be on the technique of writing two voices, but it must be approached, not as an end in itself, but as preparation for Part II, the study of the contrapuntal techniques as displayed in the two-voice Inventions. If a review of harmony is found to be necessary, Chapter 1, Theoretical Background, and Appendix A should suffice. Supplementary material for any further review of harmony should be drawn from any valid harmony text.

Three-part writing, as covered in Part III, may move directly into a study of the three-voice Fugues as presented in Part IV, omitting Chapter 24, The Sinfonias.

Under normal circumstances, Parts I and II can constitute one semester of study while Parts III and IV can be used for the second semester.

Part V is included for those teachers who are fortunate enough to have sufficient time, or gifted-enough students, to be able to use it. Appendix B falls into this category also, although parts of it may be found useful as an adjunct, and to add variety, to some of the other work, Part IV in particular.

The study of counterpoint lends itself to a more personal approach than many other theory courses do, requiring more direct contact between the teacher and the student, with resulting time-consuming discussions, demonstrations, and individual conferences. No text can take the place of the teacher, nor can it teach the course for him. Too much depends on his personal observations and experienced guidance. This text is planned so that the teacher may be released from much of the expository obligation in order that he may spend more of his time in clarification and guidance, drawing upon his own background of understanding, experience, and common sense to instill in the student a feeling for the style and the musical value of this great body of music.

Table of Contents

Part IV

Part V

To My Students
for whom, and because of whom,
this book came into being

Part I

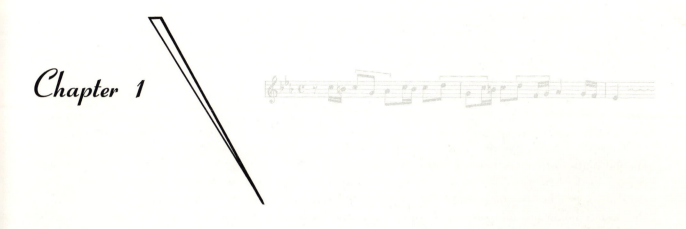

Theoretical Background

Prerequisite to the study of counterpoint in the style of the eighteenth century is a thorough knowledge of traditional harmonic practices, specifically:

1. Fundamentals (scales, keys, intervals)
2. Triads and their inversions
3. Principles of voice leading in four parts
4. Dominant dissonances and inversions
5. Subordinate (secondary) seventh chords
6. Secondary dominants
7. Non-chord (non-harmonic) tones
8. Modulation

The style of eighteenth-century counterpoint has been described as "melodized harmony" — a horizontal representation of the underlying harmonic formations. Because of the importance of harmony to a contrapuntal texture, a review of harmonic materials is in order.

HARMONIC CONTENT

The general rules for the progression of chords are the same as those learned in the study of traditional harmony.

Primary triads of a key (tonic, dominant, and subdominant) are the ones most frequently used.

EXAMPLE 1

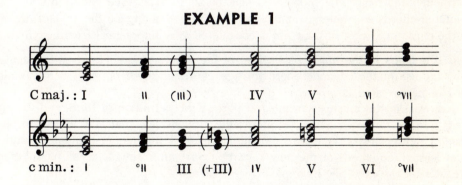

Primary triads in open notes
Most frequently used subordinate triads in stemmed black notes
Less frequently used subordinate triads in unstemmed black notes
Rarely used triads in parentheses

Subordinate triads are used sparingly, the most frequently used being the ii, and the vi.[1] The iii chord (minor) is used very rarely in a major key. The III (major) is rather common in a minor key, since it suggests the contrast of the relative major key, but the ⁺III (augmented), peculiar to the harmonic form of the minor scale, is too harsh to be very useful. The °vii triad is used in either major or minor keys as a weak substitute for the dominant. It is more frequent in minor keys.

Dissonant chords are limited almost exclusively to the chords of dominant classification (V^7, °vii^7). Subordinate seventh chords are usually restricted to the ii^7 and occasionally the vi^7, although other subordinate seventh chords may appear, but only as unessential harmonies or as a result of the use of sequence. It is extremely rare for any dissonant chord more complicated than the seventh to be found in this music; apparent ninth or thirteenth chords can better be explained as the result of non-chord tone movement essential to the melodies. The °vii°^{7} (fully diminished) is very common in minor keys, while the °vii^7 (half diminished), peculiar to major keys, is less frequently used.

Secondary dominants are common, both as triads and as seventh chords, and may be used freely. The secondary-dominant (applied-dominant) function is a temporary artificial relationship of two chords as dominant to tonic.

1) A chord is altered to take on the structure and function of a dominant (V, V^7, °vii, °vii^7) to the chord which follows it, putting temporary stress on a chord other than the tonic of the key.

EXAMPLE 2

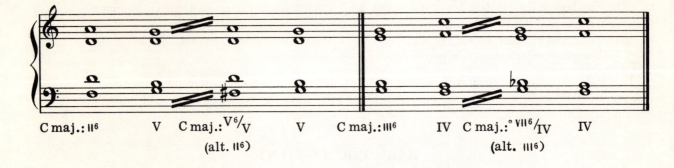

C maj.: II⁶   V   C maj.: V⁶/V   V   C maj.: III⁶   IV   C maj.: °VII⁶/IV   IV

(alt. II⁶)   (alt. III⁶)

2) The most common secondary dominant is that which is applied to the dominant of the key (the V/V), although any major or minor chord may be so stressed. (See Example 2.)
3) Other altered chords encountered in the study of the harmony of the nineteenth century are so rare in the music of Bach that their use is considered very impractical from a stylistic viewpoint.

Modulation as it appears in the music of Bach is of the simplest kind. The most frequently used is that accomplished by the use of the common chord (bridge chord or pivot chord); such modulations seldom go beyond the five next-related keys.

Modulation does exist in this music as an integral part of the definition of form, and to supply harmonic contrast, but it is possible, and in many cases preferable, to consider what may appear to be a modulation as an application of the secondary-dominant principle instead. A modulation cannot be said to be accomplished unless at least three chords of the new key are heard *after* the *point* of modulation to establish the new tonal center for the ear. (See Example 3.)

---

[1]For explanation of chord identification and secondary dominant principles as used in this text, see Appendix A.

EXAMPLE 3

G maj.: I   II⁶   V⁷
e min.:   I   IV   °VII 4/3   I⁶

(Common Chord)

Active tones are those tones that have a marked tendency to move or resolve in a certain manner. This tendency comes from the harmonic implications of the tone, either from the prevailing key or from the interval structure of the chord of which it is a part. In a logical melodic movement these tendencies are satisfied.

1) These scale steps are active, and normally resolve:

    a) 7th scale step (leading tone) resolves to tonic.
    b) 4th scale step (7th of V⁷) resolves to the mediant (3rd scale step).
    c) 2nd scale step (5th of V) resolves to tonic (sometimes to mediant).
    d) 6th scale step (7th of °vii⁷) resolves to dominant (5th scale step).

    (Note that these tones are all part of dominant harmony.)

EXAMPLE 4A

2) A tone will become active if it is altered.
    a) Tones raised from their natural pitch in the scale will acquire the tendency to ascend.
    b) Tones lowered from their natural pitch in the scale will acquire the tendency to descend.

EXAMPLE 4B

(These tones are not used at random, but are part of legitimate borrowed chords [in minor] or altered chords. Chromaticism, as such, is extremely rare in Bach.)

RHYTHMIC MOVEMENT

The rhythm found in the melodic lines of Bach's keyboard music is predominantly movement in eighth and sixteenth notes. Other note values are found frequently, but usually not as the main rhythmic movement.

When the rhythmic movement changes, as it does frequently for purposes of variety, it will usually follow this pattern:

1) A change to a slower movement will come on strong beats, or strong parts of beats.

EXAMPLE 5

2) A change to a faster movement will come on weak beats, or weak parts of beats.

EXAMPLE 6

* (Chromatic movement)

When the movement is rapid (usually in sixteenth notes), one must take care to approach the strong part of the beat smoothly (by step), especially when a chord change is also involved. Repeated notes in rapid movement should be avoided.

EXAMPLE 7

The **tie** is a rhythmic device which is extremely useful in giving a melody rhythmic independence and variety.

1) Two notes of the same value may be tied together if the first of the two is rhythmically weaker.

EXAMPLE 8

2) When the value of two tied notes is not the same, then the first of the two must be the longer.

EXAMPLE 9

Rests are useful in giving interest to the melodic line and in "ventilating" a contrapuntal texture so that it does not become too thick.

1) *Short rests* (sixteenths) may occur on the strong part of any beat. They should not occur after a non-chord tone or an active tone.

EXAMPLE 10

2) *Longer rests* are possible, but the line must definitely end before the rest is used. They will also occur on the strong part of a beat, but may be found in weaker placement also. They will not be used after a non-chord tone or an active tone.

    a) In order for a line to have a feeling of completion, it must end on the strong part of a beat and on a tone that does not need resolution.

EXAMPLE 11

ORGANIZATION OF BEATS

An obvious, but sometimes ignored, point is an understanding of the organization of beats. The following exposition may serve to bring forth an awareness of this element.

Simple Meter

The measurement of music is in the regular recurrence of patterns of strong pulses, or "beats," being opposed to, or linked with, weaker pulses, or "beats." The basic measuring unit of simple meter is one strong *beat* opposed to one weak *beat,* giving a "measure" of two-four time if the basic beat is represented to be the quarter note.

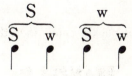

With this as a basic unit, two of them are combined, and the result is an opposition of a strong *unit* with a weaker *unit.* This is *Duple Meter.*

This grouping produces a measure of four-four time. The strong beat of the weak unit is stronger than the beat on either side, but is a little weaker than the strong beat of the strong unit. The two weak beats are about equal; if there is a difference, the weak beat of the strong unit should be favored.

$$\left(\begin{array}{c}\mathbf{4}\\\mathbf{4}\end{array}\right) \quad \overset{\text{S}}{\bullet} \quad \overset{\text{W}}{\bullet} \quad \overset{\text{S}}{\bullet} \quad \overset{\text{w}}{\bullet}$$

In combining three of these basic units in comparable notation, a measure of three-two time, with three main subdivided beats (half notes), would be produced. This, of course, could be reduced, by changing quarter notes to eighth notes, to a measure of three-four time. Here there is *one* strong unit — the first — opposed to *two* weaker units. This is *Triple Meter.*

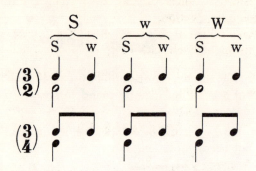

Since the second of the two weak units is further removed from the first unit, which is strong, the contrast is less, and this unit becomes slightly stronger than the first of the weak units. It is not so much overshadowed by the first unit. The weak parts of each unit will be approximately equal.

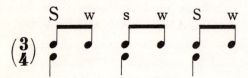

Any group of notes in any note values that fall into, or are projections of these patterns of strong and weak units have the same relative strength of their parts as the comparable beats would have in a full measure.

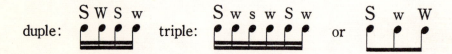

Compound Meter

This consists of an "overlay" of a measure of triple meter (usually three-four or three-eight) on each beat of a measure of simple meter. The same beat relationships exist between the first notes of each unit (the strong part of each beat) as they do in simple meter. The unit superimposed on each beat has the same comparative relationships within itself as if it were a measure of simple meter.

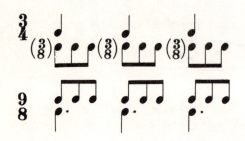

NON-CHORD TONES

The more obviously a melodic line moves along the notes of a chord in skips and leaps, the less "melodic" it becomes. Too much outlining of harmonic structures in a melodic line leads to a static feeling without the forward momentum required of a good melodic line. This problem can be overcome by concealing, delaying, or substituting for these harmonic tones certain notes which are not part of the momentary chord, non-chord tones having no harmonic implication.

The proper use of non-chord tones is one of the most important single elements of eighteenth-century counterpoint. They occur in the music of Bach with three main functional uses:

1) **Filler** — non-chord tones approached and left stepwise along a scale line to close the gap between two chord tones. (These are *passing tones*.)

EXAMPLE 12

2) **Embellishment** — non-chord tones used to ornament, or decorate, a single chord tone. (These include the *auxiliary, double auxiliary, cambiata, neighboring tone, appoggiatura,* and *escape tone*.)

EXAMPLE 13

3) **Expansion** — non-chord tones used to elongate a chord tone by tie or repetition, either before or after the principal tone. (These are the *suspension* and the *anticipation*.)

EXAMPLE 14

For the purposes of analysis, a shorthand means of identification is desirable. The following table of symbols will be used to identify non-chord tones in ensuing analyses and exercises.

Passing tone	.... P	Appoggiatura	.....................Ap
*Auiliary	......................N̶	Escape tone	......................E
Neighboring tone	...................N	Suspension	.....................S
	Anticipation	.....................A	

*This particular symbol was chosen to indicate a recognition of the fact that the auxiliary is a form of "neighboring" movement, but to differentiate between the tone approached by skip or leap and that approached by step.

An understanding of these non-chord tones is expected from the student's previous study of traditional harmony.[1]

ESSENTIAL AND UNESSENTIAL TONES

With a discussion of non-chord tones, the question of the relative importance of the notes in a melody arises.

The *essential* tones of a melody are those which form, or belong to, the harmonic implication. These notes are usually the ones which fall on the strong parts of beats, but they may appear on weaker parts of beats when they are displaced by a rest or by non-chord tones such as the suspension, appoggiatura, accented passing tone, or accented auxiliary.

EXAMPLE 15

Invention 2

The *unessential* tones of a melody are almost always in a weak rhythmic location and do little or nothing to further the harmonic implications of the melody. The suspension and appoggiatura will, however, remain unessential in spite of their strong rhythmic placement. The shape of the line and how the notes are approached and left will determine their significance, if there is any doubt.

Study Questions

1) Discuss the use of chords in eighteenth-century counterpoint.
2) Be able to describe the typical use of the secondary-dominant principle.
3) Write examples of secondary dominants to various major or minor chords in a key.
4) What is the most frequently used modulation in the music of Bach?
5) What is the difference between modulation and the secondary dominant?
6) What are "active tones," and why are they so called?
7) Give the general rules for changes in rhythmic movement.
8) What is the measurement of music?
9) What is used as a measuring unit?
10) What is duple meter?
11) What is triple meter?
12) What is compound meter?
13) What are the three main functions of non-chord tones?
14) Which non-chord tones perform these functions?
15) What are the essential tones in a melodic line?
16) What tones in a melody are considered unessential?

---

[1]A complete explanation of non-chord tones, as used in this text, is included in Appendix A to clarify and correlate for students of divergent backgrounds the various approaches and terminologies sometimes found in non-chord tone study.

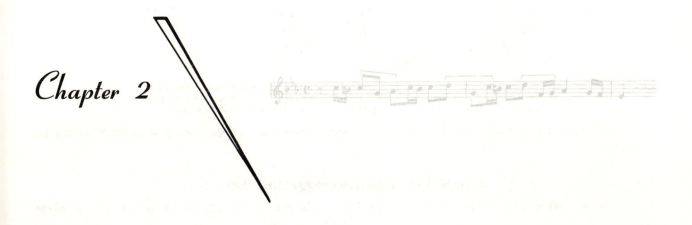

Chapter 2

Melody

The material of Bach's melodies, as, in fact, of all melodies, is movement from one tone to another. This movement may be classified as *conjunct, disjunct,* and *chromatic*.

Conjunct movement is a progression from one tone to the neighboring tone, either higher or lower, along the line of the prevailing scale. Conjunct movement is generally best, and is found to be most common in the music of Bach.

Disjunct movement is movement in skips or leaps. Movement of a *third* in either direction will be considered a *skip*, while movement in any interval larger than a third will be classified as a *leap*. This does not include the octave, which is considered to be a repetition in another register and not a leap. Disjunct movement is necessary in order to provide very desirable contrast to the more predominant stepwise movement within the melodic line.

EXAMPLE 16

W. T. C. I, Fugue I

1. Conjunct movement
2. Disjunct movement

1) Skips or leaps are best when used from the strong part of the beat to the weak between two notes belonging to the same chord.

2) Skips or leaps from weak parts of beats to strong may occur:

   a) when there is no harmonic change involved.
   b) when the harmonic change is weak or insignificant.
   c) when the skip or leap consists of the roots of two successive chords, and so would be construed as a *root progression* (usually best in the lowest line).

3) Movement in skips (thirds) is very common, and is a natural result of a melody which moves along a chord line (arpeggiation). This is very characteristic of keyboard music.

EXAMPLE 17

Invention 10

G maj.: I ——————————————— V

4) Leaps are always possible, and best when both tones are part of the same chord.

EXAMPLE 18

Invention 4

d min.: I⁶ ——————— °VII⁶ ——————— I ——————— IV

5) Almost any leap may be made to a tone which has a tendency to resolve if the direction of the leap is *opposite* to that of the natural resolution.

EXAMPLE 19A

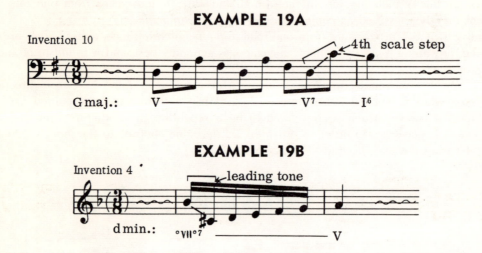

Invention 10

4th scale step

G maj.: V ——————————————— V⁷ ——— I⁶

EXAMPLE 19B

Invention 4

leading tone

d min.: °VII°⁷ ——————————— V

6) A leap to an active tone, or a tone demanding resolution, in the *same* direction as the resolution of that tone, is considered weak.

EXAMPLE 20

leading
tone

7) Wide leaps (seventh and ninth or larger) may sometimes be found in a melodic line which changes register to remain in its own *tessitura* (range). These leaps occur best immediately following an accented tone.

EXAMPLE 21A

W. T. C. I, Fugue II

EXAMPLE 21B

W. T. C. II, Fugue XVII

8) It is *not* good to skip or leap from a non-chord tone. (The escape tone is rare in Bach.)
9) The augmented fourth (diminished fifth) and the augmented second are not to be used melodically unless both notes are part of the same chord (usually within the V^7 or the $^{\circ}vii^{\circ7}$ only).

EXAMPLE 22

Invention 9

c min.:   i ——— $^{\circ}VII^{\circ7}$ ——— (V)   i

10) After a leap, the melody should change direction.

EXAMPLE 23

W. T. C. I, Fugue II

a) A melody may skip and leap along the chord line in the same direction but will very rarely exceed an octave and never exceed a tenth without changing direction.

EXAMPLE 24

W. T. C. I, Fugue X

A change of harmony will usually call for stepwise movement in the melodic line, or at the least, a change of direction.

b) It is possible to move on conjunctly in the same direction after a leap if the melody then changes direction.

EXAMPLE 25

W. T. C. I, Fugue VIII

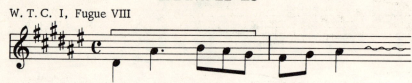

c) The melody does not need to change direction after a leap if the second note of the leap is sufficiently stressed:

(1) by being longer than the notes surrounding it,

EXAMPLE 26

(2) by being repeated or tied,

EXAMPLE 27

(3) or being embellished with an auxiliary (or a trill, or mordent).

EXAMPLE 28

11) Too many skips or leaps in a melody tend to make the harmonic element too strong, and the melodic flow thus may be interrupted, or at least slowed down.

EXAMPLE 29

Invention 10

12) On the other hand, some skips and leaps are valuable, not only for the sake of melodic variety (or contrast), but also to help solidify the harmonic implications that are needed.

EXAMPLE 30

Invention 11

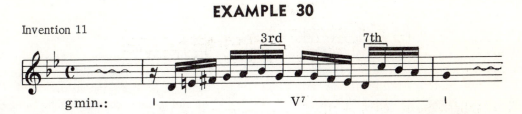

Chromatic movement occurs in a progression where the normal intervals of the diatonic scale are made smaller by the use of accidentals. True chromatic movement is one which uses two notes of the *same letter name* with one of them raised or lowered by means of an accidental. This type of movement is rare in the music of Bach. When it is found, it is usually in slow rhythmic movement with notes moving in values of a full beat.

EXAMPLE 31

W. T. C. I, Fugue XII

* (Chromatic Movement)

1) A chromatic movement (*not* chromaticism as part of an altered chord) will usually be approached in the same direction as the inflection, and continue in the same direction.

EXAMPLE 32

2) A fussy, complicated line results when another tone is inserted between the notes of a chromatic movement, and is best avoided.

EXAMPLE 33

MELODY AND HARMONY

A melodic line is a horizontal projection of the harmonic structures through which it passes. Conversely, it must be kept in mind that any melodic movement in intervals larger than a half or whole step is heard as a partial (or complete) outline of a chord with which our musical background makes us familiar, so *a melody also implies the chords from which it has been derived.*

EXAMPLE 34

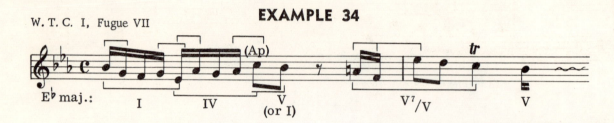

Chord changes should not occur on weak beats, or weak parts of beats. In other words, the harmony should not be "syncopated." Since skips and leaps imply chords, then a skip or leap from the weak part of the beat to a stronger one would tend to imply this syncopation, and there would be an undesirable displacement of the chord change to a weak part of the beat. Normally, a chord will not be held over into a beat stronger than the one on which it began.

MELODIC UNITY AND VARIETY

The strongest unifying feature in a melody (as in all Art) is that of **repetition.** There are two kinds of repetition possible in a melodic line:

1) Repeated rhythmic pattern.

EXAMPLE 35

The use of this device must be tempered with reason. This example shows more than the usual number of rhythmic repetitions. Two or three would generally be considered to be enough.

2) Repeated melodic figure.

EXAMPLE 36

The danger of melodic repetition lies in monotony — a static feeling — so it must be used sparingly. It halts the melodic progression.

Sequence is a form of melodic repetition, but on different scale steps — more correctly, a *recurrence* — and is of vital importance in this style. There is *unity* in the repetition of the rhythmic pattern and also in the duplication of the outline of the melodic figure, with the added element of *variety* in the change of pitch for each repetition.

EXAMPLE 37

Invention 1

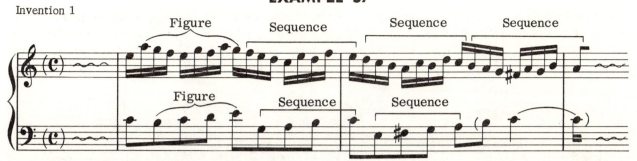

(This example actually shows two sequence patterns occurring at the same time. Each is independent of the other.)

The pattern of sequential recurrence is regular, the figures moving usually:

1) by step,

EXAMPLE 38

Invention 4

2) or by thirds.

EXAMPLE 39

Invention 14

3) Occasionally, they may recur in fourths or fifths, but here harmonic implications can become so strong as to overshadow the purely melodic function of the sequence.

EXAMPLE 40

Invention 7

As is often the case, too much of something may lead to trouble — in this case, monotony. Therefore, in general practice, such patterns are limited to *three recurrences* of the figure. (Sometimes as many as four may be found, but usually with a short figure.) At least *two* recurrences are usually considered essential to the establishment of the pattern, except, perhaps, in the case of a rather long figure of which one recurrence might be sufficient.

Contrast is necessary in any melodic line as the antidote for monotony. Therefore, the usual practice is found to be an alternation of melodic and rhythmic ideas, or an opposition of them.

    1) Alternation:

EXAMPLE 41

W. T. C. I, Fugue XIII

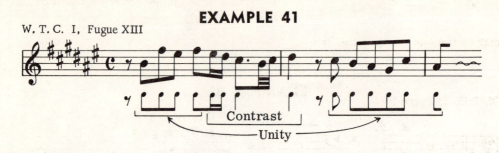

    2) Opposition:

EXAMPLE 42

W. T. C. I, Fugue XI

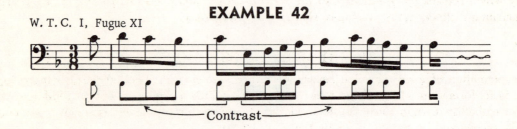

MELODIC SHAPE AND FORM

The most obvious visible characteristic of a melodic line is its shape. It has direction. It goes somewhere, and generally returns. The high point (or sometimes the low point) of a melody is called the *climax*. This is essential to the expressiveness and balance of the line. It supplies a kind of "tension" to which the melody builds, and from which it releases. The most common melodic shapes or curves are:

    1) Climax at midpoint, or a little beyond.

EXAMPLE 43

W. T. C. I, Fugue XIV

    2) Climax at the end.

EXAMPLE 44

Sinfonia 15

    3) Climax at the beginning.

EXAMPLE 45

Goldberg Variations, no. 18

4) Climax as the *low* point of the line.

EXAMPLE 46

W. T. C. I, Fugue XVI

A melody which returns too frequently to the same point of climax loses its feeling of shape and direction. For maximum effectiveness, a climax should occur only once.

PRIMARY MELODIC MOVEMENT

A close examination of a melodic line reveals that there are certain tones which are more important than others in its formation. Many of the tones seem to have little purpose except to reinforce, elongate, or otherwise embellish certain more stable fundamental tones. This characteristic may sometimes be more quickly recognized by the ear than by the eye.

These fundamental melodic tones will usually lie on the strong parts of beats, or may follow immediately after a suspension, or a short rest. (See Chapter 1, page 10.) Usually, in a melodic line, these tones will be found to form a smooth, fundamental movement, most often in stepwise relationship, serving as the primary melodic progression around which expressive melodic peregrinations may occur.

1) In an arpeggiated triad, one tone (often the root) may be the primary tone, with the other tones serving to *reinforce* it.

EXAMPLE 47

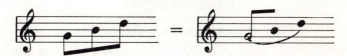

(Open note indicates primary tone. Black note heads indicate reinforcing tones with slur indicating their relationship to the primary tone.)

2) Stepwise patterns may be used to *expand* a primary tone.

EXAMPLE 48

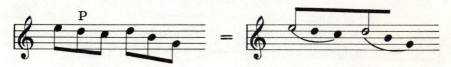

(Successive primary tones will be stemmed to a continuous beam.)

3) Expansion is also evident in the suspension and anticipation.

EXAMPLE 49

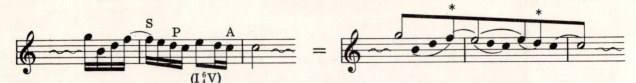

*The F and D also serve as filling movements between two primary notes,
so are stemmed to indicate their importance.

4) *Embellishing movements* such as auxiliary or neighboring tones are common.

EXAMPLE 50A

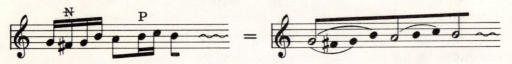

EXAMPLE 50B

5) Often subordinate melodic relationships may exist for a few notes, either as suggested pedal points, or as stepwise movement. The importance of these secondary movements can be indicated by stemming and beaming them separately from the primary tones.

EXAMPLE 51

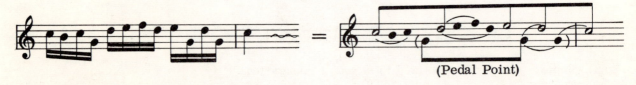

(Pedal Point)

6) The graphic indications in this type of melodic analysis must show relationships clearly and logically. A certain amount of originality is often necessary to make the graph as clear as possible.
7) The vivid picture of the structure of a melodic line such a graphic analysis presents is extremely revealing of the true relationship and relative importance of the notes within a melodic line, as well as the methods by which direction and coherence may be achieved.

EXAMPLE 52

Sinfonia 4

Study Questions

1) What three kinds of melodic movement are found in melodic lines?
2) Discuss their uses, and their comparative importance.
3) What are the specific principles for handling skips and leaps?
4) What is the relationship of a melodic line to its harmonic background?
5) What is said concerning the placement of the chords of a harmonic progression?
6) How is unity obtained in a melodic line?
7) Discuss the use and importance of variety or contrast in a melodic line.
8) What is a melodic climax, and where may it occur?

Critical Analysis of Melodic Lines

1) The following melodies are to be analyzed in the light of this Chapter and Chapter 1.
2) Errors or weaknesses found are to be explained.
3) Numbered beats are for convenient reference in discussion.
4) Each melody is to be examined as a whole, and minutely. Aural examination can prove helpful as well.

EXERCISE 1

Exercises for Writing

Write melodic lines using the given harmonic progression as background.

1) Use three staves. Copy chords on the lower staff.
2) Select a time signature. Place chords in measures so that important chords fall on strong beats (especially the final tonic).
3) Sketch a melodic outline on the middle staff by selecting notes from the given chords which will form a smooth, logical progression. End with the root of the tonic chord.
4) On the upper staff, elaborate this sketch into a Bach-type melody by adding non-chord tones and other notes belonging to the given chords, following all the principles in the text.
5) Play the melody with and without the harmonic background as a check. (Don't worry about doubling.)
6) The melody must make sense melodically and imply the given harmony clearly.

MODEL OF PROCEDURE:

MODEL 1

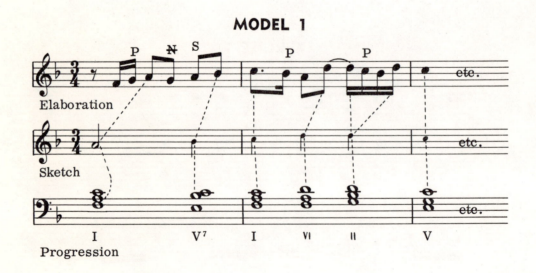

PROGRESSIONS:

EXERCISE 2

Graphic Analysis

Analyze several of the following melodic excerpts in the manner of Example 52.

1) Invention 5 — upper voice, measure 1 through first beat of measure 4.
2) Invention 9 — both voices, measure 1 through first beat of measure 4.
3) Invention 11 — upper voice, last six measures (register changes).
4) Sinfonia 10 — upper voice, last seven measures and one beat.
5) W.T.C. I, Fugue VIII — middle voice, to third beat of third measure.
6) W.T.C. I, Fugue VIII — upper voice, last five measures.
7) W.T.C. I, Fugue XII — upper voice, measure 22 to measure 29, first beat (register changes).
8) W.T.C. I, Fugue XXIV — upper voice, measure 65, beat three, to measure 70, first beat.

Chapter 3

The Melodic Minor

In minor keys, the harmonic form of the scale is the source of the accepted, and expected, harmonic structures. However, in using this form of the scale to produce a melody, composers continually encounter the awkward movement between the 6th and 7th scale steps (low 6th, raised 7th) which is an augmented second. Stylistically, this interval is not acceptable within a melodic line except under the specific conditions stated in Chapter 2, page 13. This "unmelodic" element leads composers to the use of the *melodic* form of the minor scale for the formation of melodic lines because it eliminates the augmented second by the use of accidentals. This procedure may produce some changes in chord formations, but generally these are not used as essential harmonies. It is to be remembered that the *harmonic* roots are still in the harmonic form of the scale.

The typical use of the materials of the melodic minor scale is illustrated by the following examples:

1) Raised 6th and 7th scale steps in an ascending pattern.

EXAMPLE 53

a min.: V⁷ ——————— I

2) Lowered 7th and 6th scale steps in a descending pattern.

EXAMPLE 54

c min.: °VII ——————— I   7   6

Further qualification of specific uses of the inflections found in the melodic minor is necessary. The importance of a strong harmonic background in this style dictates that the harmonic functions not be destroyed, and that accidentals used to avoid the augmented second in patterns involving the 6th and 7th scale steps in succession depend not entirely on direction of movement of the melodic line, but much more on the *essential* notes of the harmony, which should adhere to the harmonic form of the minor scale.

It is necessary to make the needed melodic adjustments only on *unessential* tones (those not belonging to the chord) which must agree in spelling with the essential tones of the harmony of the moment.

1) 6TH SCALE STEP AS NON-CHORD TONE

In a passage in which the harmony is *dominant*, the *ascending* form of the melodic minor scale is usually used in either direction, allowing the use of the raised leading tone, which is characteristic of the dominant chord.

EXAMPLE 55A

EXAMPLE 55B

2) 7TH SCALE STEP AS NON-CHORD TONE

In a passage in which the harmony is *subdominant*, the *descending* form of the melodic minor scale is usually used in either direction.

EXAMPLE 56

3) 6TH AND 7TH SCALE STEPS AS PASSING TONES

a) During *tonic* harmonies, the *ascending* form is usually used in an upward passage, and the *descending* form is used in a downward movement.

EXAMPLE 57

b) In certain instances where a noticeable cross-relation would exist in the melodic line between a raised 6th scale step in an ascending pattern within tonic harmony, and a lowered 6th scale step in a subdominant harmony immediately following, the descending form may be used within the tonic harmony, even in an ascending pattern, in order to respect the typical quality of the minor subdominant.

EXAMPLE 58

4) In other cases, the most significant harmonic tone will govern the notation.

Other accidentals appearing in a melodic line which may become confused with the uses of the melodic minor are accounted for as follows:

1) The raised lower auxiliary.
2) Alterations used to form functional chords, such as secondary dominants, and other tones altered to avoid the augmented second with the tones of these chords.
3) Within extended scale passages, passing tones sometimes take their inflection from the key of the momentary chord.
4) The final judgment lies with the ear, which will recognize the proper (or improper) use of accidentals quite readily if only given a chance.

Students often become involved in the use of melodic minor, and in this connection it might be well to point out that perfectly good minor melodies are written which do not involve the use of the 6th and 7th scale steps in succession. It is not necessary to avoid or fear this progression, however, if reasonable care is taken not to use it in excess or without thought.

Study Questions

1) From which form of the minor scale is the basic harmonic vocabulary derived?
2) What stylistic problem is encountered in melodic lines within this scale?
3) How is this overcome?
4) Differentiate between the specific uses of the harmonic and melodic forms of the minor scale.
5) Be able to discuss fully, and write examples to illustrate, the three specific applications of the melodic minor.

Critical Analysis of Minor Melodies

In the following exercises, find errors or weaknesses in the use of the melodic minor and rewrite correctly.

EXERCISE 3

Exercises for Writing

Write melodic lines through the following harmonies in the manner of Chapter 2, page 22, following the principles of the proper use of the melodic minor.

PROGRESSIONS:

EXERCISE 4

Chapter 4

The Association of Two Voices

The simplest form of counterpoint is that in two voices. It is less complicated than when more voices are used, but in some ways it is the most difficult, particularly in the matter of maintaining interest with the limited degree of variety at the composer's disposal. Here the individual melodic line is of first concern while at the same time constant consideration must be given to the relationship of the two melodies to one another.

CLASSIFICATION OF INTERVALS

For organization, the harmonic intervals which occur between the two voices will be classified according to their apparent frequency and usefulness. This classification is based on a study of the music of Bach and the writings of the theorists of the period.

Consonances

These intervals are the most frequently used and are considered to be the most pleasing.

1) PRIMARY CONSONANCES

        Major 3rd — Minor 6th

        Minor 3rd — Major 6th

Use: Anytime, in any rhythmic placement, and in almost any order or connection.

Restrictions: Only four to six of a kind should be used in succession in order to avoid loss of independence of voices.

2) SECONDARY CONSONANCES

        Perfect 8ve (or unison)

        Perfect 5th

Use: Very common, but subject to restrictions.

Restrictions:

    a) Cannot occur in succession (8-8 or 5-5).

    b) Cannot be interchanged (8-5 or 5-8), except rarely in the repetition of the same chord.

    c) The perfect octave should not be approached in similar motion in both voices if the upper part makes a leap (hidden octaves).

    d) The perfect fifth should not be approached in similar motion with a leap in either part (hidden fifths), except possibly in chord repetition.

Dissonances

These intervals are used frequently, but their use is carefully governed by specific conditions based on their harmonic or melodic characteristics.

1) MILD DISSONANCES

> Diminished 5th — Augmented 4th
>
> Diminished 7th — Augmented 2nd
>
> Minor 7th — Major 2nd

Use: These intervals owe their value to the harmonic fact that they all belong to chords with dominant characteristics — the V^7, the $^\circ vii$, and the $^\circ vii^7$, and also chords of the same construction as these which function as secondary dominants. Their best use is in connection with primary consonances wherever possible, where their natural melodic and harmonic tendencies can best be fulfilled. They should be approached as smoothly as possible.

Restrictions:

> *a*) Cannot be used in succession or interchanged.
>
> *b*) May be used with secondary consonances, but with caution as regards voice leading (hidden intervals).
>
> *c*) Should not be approached by a wide leap in either part except, possibly, in chord repetition.

2) STRONG DISSONANCES

> Major 7th — Minor 2nd
>
> Perfect 4th (usually implying a six-four chord)

Use:

> *a*) Almost exclusively as a result of the use of non-chord tones.
>
> *b*) The perfect fourth may appear in connection with other intervals in chord repetition (arpeggiation of a chord in both voices).

Restrictions:

> *a*) Cannot be used in succession or interchanged.
>
> *b*) Must be used with extreme caution and be approached and left as smoothly as possible.

TWO-VOICE WRITING

When two voices are combined into a contrapuntal texture, there are formed, coincidentally, vertical intervals between the two melodies which have strong harmonic significance. These intervals imply, or represent, chords. Some of these implications may be indistinct, as in the case of a third or a sixth, both of which could represent at least two harmonic possibilities.

EXAMPLE 59

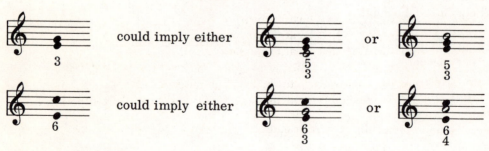

In other cases, such as the fourth or the fifth, it is probable that only one chord could be construed.

EXAMPLE 60

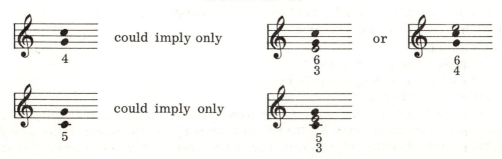

Where doubt exists, the context will usually supply the answer. In other words, one of the chords would make a better progression than the other. Other melodic notes before or after the doubtful interval will also tend to clarify the implication.

The factor of rhythmic placement will often help to determine the implication of the interval, since the interval at the stronger rhythmic location will usually exert the strongest influence on the ear.

Harmonic progression is necessarily clear and simple so as not to disturb or overshadow the movement of the melodic lines. Chords are usually at least one beat in length, and may continue for as much as a measure.

As a general rule, a chord will not be held over into a beat stronger than the one on which it began. The harmony should be changed when moving into a strong beat.

Study Questions

1) Name the consonant intervals.
2) What is their best use?
3) What restrictions apply to the use of consonant intervals?
4) What are the dissonant intervals?
5) How are they best used?
6) What restrictions apply to the use of dissonant intervals?
7) What is meant by an "implied" harmony?
8) Summarize the harmonic content of this music.

Harmonic and Melodic Analysis

The following two-voice excerpts are to be copied and analyzed with chord numerals and non-chord tone symbols. They are not necessarily complete. They may not begin and end on the tonic chord. They may sometimes appear in a different key than the original key of the piece.

1) Invention 5 — measure 1 to first beat of measure 5.
2) Invention 9 — measure 1 to first beat of measure 4.
3) Invention 2 — measure 3 to first beat of measure 7.
4) Invention 7 — measure 15 to first beat of measure 18 (involves pedal-point).
5) W.T.C. I, Prelude II — measure 1 to first beat of measure 12.
6) W.T.C. I, Fugue III — third beat of measure 33 to third beat of measure 39.
7) W.T.C. I, Fugue X — measure 32 to end.
8) W.T.C. I, Fugue XV — measure 73 to first beat of measure 77.

Chapter 5

Note-Against-Note (First Species) Counterpoint

True First Species counterpoint is quite rare for any extended passage in the keyboard music of Bach. This is due to the fact that the problem of making each voice independent is most easily solved by the use of rhythmic contrast which, of course, is lacking in this species since both voices are moving note for note. However, there are short passages to be found, and at these times the association of the voices is governed by the following principles:

1) Primary consonances are used almost exclusively.
2) If other intervals are used, they will appear on weak beats, or weak parts of beats.
3) Non-chord tones may be used if they do not disturb the desired harmonic implications. The passing tone, the auxiliary, and the double auxiliary, on occasion, are the most frequently used non-chord tones in this species, although the suspension and the neighbor tone may be found under certain conditions. They should be used rarely and with caution.
4) It is possible that mild dissonances may appear on strong beats or fractions, if the harmony is obviously dominant (or has dominant function).
5) In an arpeggiated figure, exceptional intervals may appear on strong beats, or fractions, if they belong to the chord and the harmony is clear and part of an acceptable progression.
6) Note that even non-chord tones usually form good intervals.

First Species Examples

EXAMPLE 61A

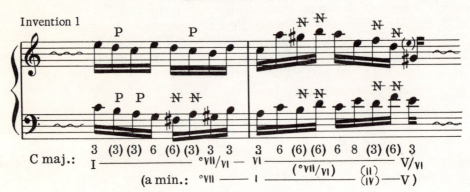

In these, and the examples which follow, numerals in parentheses designate intervals formed by one or more non-chord tones, and are *unessential*; numerals in circles designate dissonant intervals which belong to the momentary chord and are, therefore, *essential dissonances*.

EXAMPLE 61B

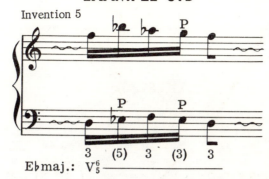

EXAMPLE 62

EXAMPLE 63

(1) Fourth on strong fraction
(2) Diminished fifth (augmented fourth) on strong fraction

Exercises in First Species Counterpoint

1) WITH GIVEN LINE:

a) Using one or two staves as needed, add a line to the given line according to the principles of First Species.

b) Determine the harmonic background implied by the given line. At certain points, the specific chord may be obscure. Indicate all possibilities.

c) Begin the added voice on a good interval within the tonic chord.

d) If the added voice is the lower part, be certain that it ends on the root of the tonic chord.

e) Indicate the final implied harmony with numerals; identify all intervals, and indicate whether essential or unessential; identify non-chord tones with symbols.

f) Do not use repeated notes.

g) The given lines may be transposed to a higher or lower register to allow adding a voice in the opposite relationship.

EXERCISE 5

2) WITH GIVEN HARMONIC PROGRESSION:

a) Write two-voice counterpoint in First Species through the following general harmonic backgrounds.

b) Distribute the chords of the progressions over several measures in rhythmic arrangement. Place the final tonic on a strong beat.

c) Write good melodic lines that will agree according to the rules of two-voice writing and imply the desired harmony.

d) Most inversions are not indicated because they will depend upon the movement of the voices.

e) End with the root of the final chord in the lower voice.

Major Key:

(1) I I⁶ IV ii V I

(2) I IV I V IV V vi

(3) I V I IV I vi V/V V I

Minor Key:

(1) i °ii⁶ V i VI iv V i

(2) i iv °ii III VI °ii V i

(3) i V i iv °ii i °vii i

Chapter 6

Two-Against-One (Second Species) Counterpoint

Two notes against one is the most common movement of two voices to be found in Bach's keyboard music. Here, more freedom in the use of non-chord tones and of intervals in general is allowable, the prime objective being to produce smoothly moving, symmetrical melodic lines.

1) Primary consonances are still preferred on strong beats, or fractions, but this is not necessary if the melodic movement is smooth and the harmony is clear and correct.

2) All non-chord tones may be used, but still preferred are the weaker ones such as the passing tone and the auxiliary.
   a) Repeated notes should not be used.
   b) The neighboring tone and the escape tone should be avoided.

3) Statements four and five in First Species are still good. (See Chapter 5.)

4) Symmetry of line begins to become of primary importance.
   a) The use of sequence of figures comprising one or two beats is desirable and lines should be planned to use this device. In general, no more than *three sequences* of a figure should be used in succession.
   b) When a voice is moving rapidly (usually sixteenth notes), it is best to move into beats by step, unless a strong harmonic progression is involved, or unless the chord remains the same.
   c) Skips and leaps are best used from strong to weak parts of beats and not vice versa except when the chord does not change.

5) It is desirable to change the chord on strong beats in a regular pattern. A chord which is begun on a weak beat should not be allowed to carry over into a strong beat.

Second Species Examples

EXAMPLE 64

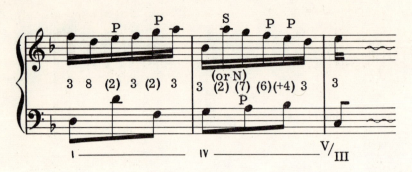

EXAMPLE 65

EXAMPLE 66

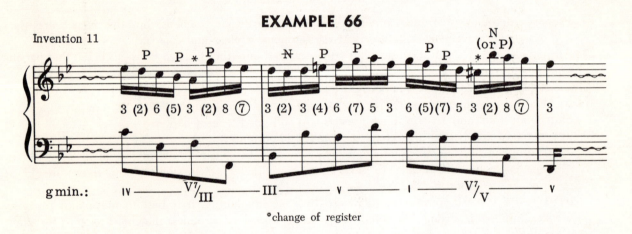

*change of register

EXAMPLE 67

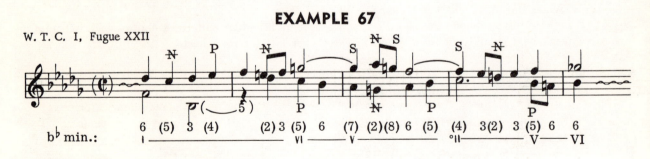

True three-against-one movement is so rare and incidental in the music of Bach that it will suffice to say that it is classified as an elaboration of Second Species, and as such is considered to have only *one* essential note per beat, the other two being handled as reinforcing chord tones, or as typical non-chord tone movement. This will differ from the next species, as will be seen.

Exercises in Second Species Counterpoint

1) WITH GIVEN LINE:
    a) Add a voice to the given line in sixteenth notes. Indicate chords, intervals, and non-chord tones as in Chapter 5.
    b) Transpose lines to the opposite register and add a voice in the same manner.
    c) Keep in mind that skips from strong to weak imply a chord.
    d) The suggested harmonies are not the only possible chords which may appear.
    e) Try to retain the same *category* of chord (IV-ii; V-°vii; etc.).
    f) Other harmonic formations that may occur should be incidental to the main harmonic background.

EXERCISE 6

2) WITH GIVEN HARMONIC PROGRESSION:
    a) Write two-voice counterpoint in Second Species through the following general harmonic backgrounds. Identify intervals and non-chord tones as before.
    b) Distribute the chords of the progressions over several measures in good rhythmic arrangement.
    c) Write good melodic lines that will agree according to the rules of two-voice writing, and imply the desired harmony.
    d) Inversions are not indicated because they will depend on voice movement.
    e) Harmonic substitution may be made within the same category of chord.
    f) Keep rhythmic relationships the same throughout.

Major Key:

   (1) I IV I vi ii V I

   (2) I iii IV I IV V/V V I

   (3) I V vi ii iii IV V I

Minor Key:

   (1) i iv °ii $^+$III VI °vii/V V i

   (2) i V i iv ii V i

   (3) i iv i V i °ii VI V^7/III III

Chapter 7

First and Second Species in Combination

The governing factor in combining First and Second Species is variety. It would be monotonous to continue a whole piece in one rhythmic relationship. The independence of voices requires that the rhythmic relationship of the voices be varied frequently to avoid overemphasis of either voice.

The principles set down in Chapters 5 and 6 for the handling of First Species and of Second Species counterpoint are used as needed according to the rhythmic relationship of the voices.

Example of First and Second Species Combined

EXAMPLE 68

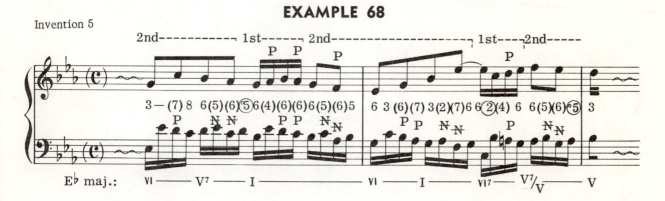

Exercises in First and Second Species Counterpoint

1) With Given Melody and Rhythmic Pattern:
   a) Determine the harmonic background implied by the given melodic line.
   b) Write the second voice in the given rhythmic pattern reinforcing and ornamenting this harmonic progression.
   c) Analyze non-chord tones and keep track of intervals.
   d) Be alert to possible use of sequential patterns.

EXERCISE 7

2) WITH GIVEN MELODY:

    a) Add a second voice above or below the given melody in varied rhythm, according to the principles of First and Second Species.

    b) Keep the added voice rhythmically and melodically independent from the given voice, but reinforce its harmonic implications.

    c) The rhythmic movement of both voices should add up to a steady composite rhythm of eighth or sixteenth notes.

    d) Avoid "dead" spots, rhythmically.

    e) Look for opportunities for using similar rhythmic and melodic ideas in the added voice to those in the given voice.

EXERCISE 8

Chapter 8

Four-Against-One (Third Species) Counterpoint

In movement of four notes against one greater freedom is allowed, yet care must be taken not to let the greater movement in one voice imply harmonies which are not desirable or fitting.

1) All non-chord tones may now be used, except that the escape tone is extremely rare and the neighboring tone must be used with caution so as not to imply undesirable harmonies.

2) The anticipation will be found only in a perfect authentic cadence at the end of a section, or at the end of the piece, and will be used only in the upper voice and anticipating the root of the final chord of the cadence.

3) Repeated notes may appear when the second note forms a suspension.

4) Symmetry of line and sequence are desirable characteristics of the melodic line.

5) Stepwise movement into beats is best in rapid movement, unless the chord is repeated.

6) The *cambiata* is a figure which becomes more characteristic of the more rapid melodic movement of the species. In its classic form, it is a four-note figure of which the second and third notes are usually dissonant, the melodic pattern being down a step, down a third, up a step.

EXAMPLE 69

5 (4) (2) 3

(The reverse [inversion] of this figure is extremely rare.)

It is desirable to re-examine essential and unessential notes (Chapter 1, page 10), and the organization of beats (Chapter 1, page 7). In this species, one should note the existence of two relatively strong pulses per beat as a reduction of a four-beat measure. This can influence the proper use of non-chord tones.

Examples of Third Species

Third Species is not generally used for any extended length of time because of the obviously static character of one of the voices, which is particularly dangerous when only two voices are used, since it leads to a subordination of one of the voices if carried on too long.

EXAMPLE 70

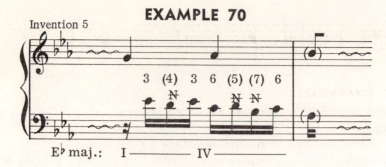

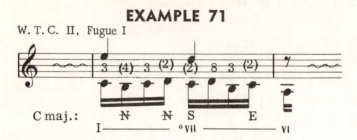

EXAMPLE 71

(The unusual appearance of non-chord tones in this example results from the fact that the lower voice is part of a series of sequences.)

EXAMPLE 72

Exercises in Third Species Counterpoint

1) WITH GIVEN LINE:
   a) Add a voice to the given line in Third Species counterpoint.
   b) Indicate chord background, and identify intervals and non-chord tones.

EXERCISE 9

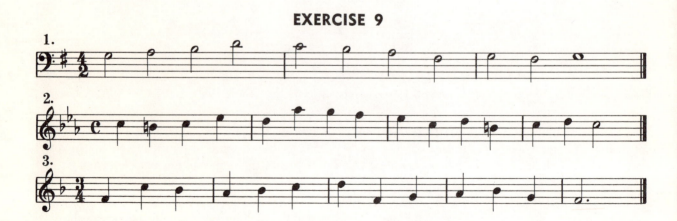

4.

2) WITH HARMONIC PROGRESSION:

  a) Write two voices implying these harmonies, alternating note values between voices to produce continuous four-against-one movement.

  b) No one voice should continue with slow movement for too long a time.

  c) An occasional Second Species movement may be allowed for variety, but only for a beat or two.

  d) First Species (both voices in sixteenth notes) may appear for no more than one beat.

  Major Key:
  > (1) I IV ii V IV^6 V$^6_5$ I
  > (2) I V vi ii IV V^7 I

  Minor Key:
  > (1) i iv °ii V i VI V^7 i
  > (2) i °ii V VI IV °ii V^7 i

Chapter 9

Counterpoint with Tied Notes (Fourth Species)

Fourth Species is concerned with the proper use of tied notes. The *tie* is a valuable device for giving independence to a melodic line, and also for escaping monotony in rhythmic patterns.

1) The tie should be made from a weak beat, or fraction, to a strong beat, or fraction.
2) The value of the first of the two notes will be as long as, or longer than, the value of the second note. The first note should not be shorter than the second. The most common ratio for two tied notes is 2:1, although 4:1 is frequent.
3) A tie which produces a dissonance on the strong beat, or fraction, is called a *dissonant tie,* or suspension. A tie which produces a consonance on the strong beat, or fraction, is called a *consonant tie.*
    a) DISSONANT TIE (SUSPENSION)
    Movement away from the dissonant note must be by step to a consonance. An exception may be made, however, if the dissonance is part of a dominant seventh chord (an essential dissonance), in which case the note may skip or leap to another note of the same chord. In this instance, the voice usually turns back so that the original note of resolution for the dissonance is arrived at within a beat, or on the next beat at the latest.
    b) CONSONANT TIE
    Movement away from the consonant note may be either by stepwise motion, often to a nonchord tone, or by skip or leap, moving to a chord tone.
4) In either kind of tie, the first note of the two tied notes must be consonant (a part of the momentary chord).
5) Frequently a dotted note, or a syncopation, may be found substituting for a tie which would have the same value.

Examples of Fourth Species

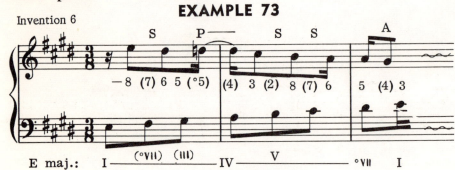

EXAMPLE 73

EXAMPLE 74

Invention 9

f min.: I ——————— VI ——— °II ————

EXAMPLE 75

Invention 13

a min.: I ——————— V⁷ ——————— I

EXAMPLE 76

W. T. C. I, Fugue I

G maj.: V⁷ ——— VI ——— V ——— V⁷ ——————— I

Exercises in Fourth Species Counterpoint

1) Add a line to each of the given lines, using ties from weak to strong as much as possible beginning after a rest.
2) An occasional lapse into Second Species for no more than a beat and a half is allowable to move the line to a better position.
3) Identify all intervals and mark the strong note of each tie as "C" for consonant or "D" for dissonant.
4) Harmony will be important only as it affects the key and the first and last notes of the added line.
5) Both voices will end with the same note value.

MODEL 2

EXERCISE 10

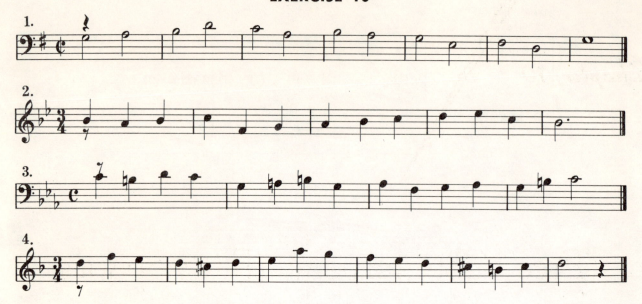

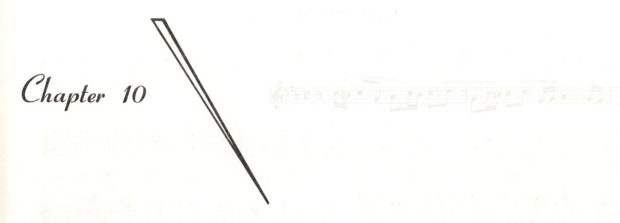

Chapter 10

"Free" Counterpoint (Fifth Species)

Fifth Species does not present a separate problem but rather is concerned with the use of all the other species. Therefore, there are no separate rules or principles governing this species, as it is a combination of the principles thus far covered. The one underlying principle of this species is a logical and artistic balance of the combining of the other species.

1) The most common species used will be Second Species — two notes against one.
2) Note-against-note (First Species), and four-against-one (Third Species) are less commonly used, but when movement in one of these species occurs, then it will be governed by the principles of that species.
3) Tied notes, both consonant and dissonant, are, as has been said, invaluable in lending independence to a melodic line, and will be governed by the principles of Fourth Species.

Example of Free Counterpoint (Fifth Species)

EXAMPLE 77

Exercises in Free Counterpoint

1) MELODY WITH RHYTHMIC PATTERN GIVEN:
   - *a*) The rhythm is given for the second voice.
   - *b*) Make ties suspensions where possible.
   - *c*) Indicate harmonic background and non-chord tones.
   - *d*) Watch for opportunities to use sequences.

EXERCISE 11

2) RHYTHMIC PATTERN ONLY FOR BOTH VOICES:
   - *a*) Chords are general. Position is optional.
   - *b*) Exercises are given with chords of a major key. They may be easily and profitably converted to minor.
   - *c*) Take advantage of similar rhythmic groupings to use similar melodic lines in both voices.
   - *d*) Make ties suspensions whenever possible.
   - *e*) Identify non-chord tones.

EXERCISE 12

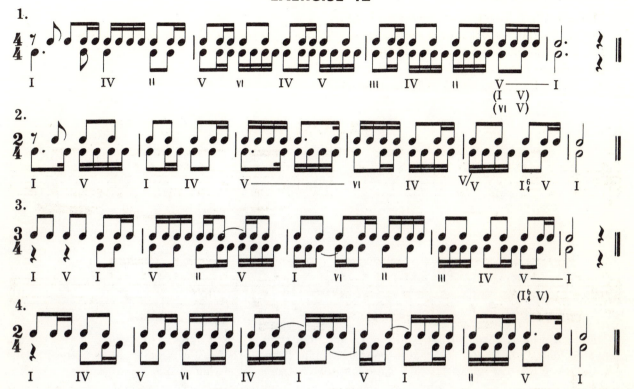

1.

I · · · IV · II · V · VI · IV · V · III · IV · II · V——I
(I   V)
(VI   V)

2.

I · V · I · IV · V————VI · IV · V/V · I⁶₄ V · I

3.

I · V · I · V · II · V · I · VI · II · III · IV · V——I
(I⁶₄ V)

4.

I · IV · V · VI · IV · I · V · I · II · V · I

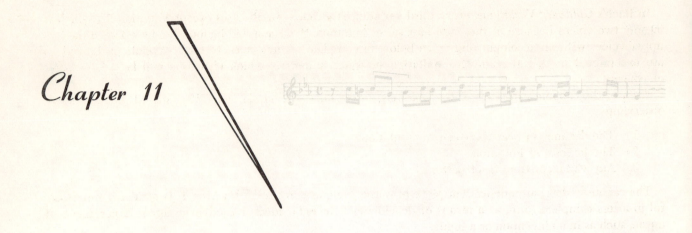

Chapter 11

The Canon

One of the strongest characteristics of the contrapuntal style is *imitation,* or reproducing in one voice a motive or figure which another has just completed. The *canon* is the most extreme example of this process.

A canon is a piece of music in which the motives and figures appearing in one voice are reproduced in another continuously at a fixed interval of time and pitch from the first.

1) The first voice is called the "leader."
2) The imitative voice is called the "follower."
3) A canon is identified, or described, by the melodic interval between the voices and also by the length of time (in beats) between the entrances. The following example is a canon "at the octave, after three beats."

EXAMPLE 78

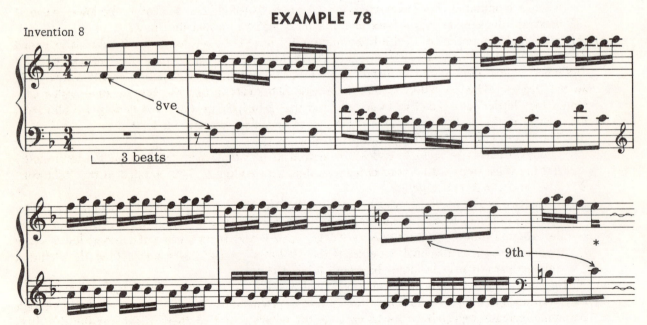

*From here for the next nine beats, the original interval of imitation has been increased from an octave to a ninth; therefore, it would be said that the canon has ceased, and strict imitation has been substituted for it.

50

In Bach's *Goldberg Variations,* every third variation is a canon. In all cases except Variation 27, which is in only two voices because of the wide interval of imitation, the canon will be found to be between the two upper voices with an accompanying voice below to complete a three-voice texture. (Variations 12 and 15 are exceptional in that they involve imitation in contrary motion, which technique will be a later point of concern).

Each of the canonic variations of the *Goldberg Variations* (except 12 and 15) should be examined, observing:

1) The distance in beats between the imitations.
2) The interval of imitation.
3) Any variances from a set pattern.

The canon exists as an independent piece of music, complete in itself. However, it is generally more useful in a less complete form, as a means of developing a melodic idea or motive within a larger piece of music, such as in an invention or a fugue.

There are other types of canons which involve more complicated devices of imitation (Variations 12 and 15 above, as an example), but most of these are too complex for practical development in the comparatively simple structure of the invention.

Writing a Canon

In writing a canon, all principles of melodic line, voice leading, chord progression, and the association of two voices must be observed.

1) Select a short melodic idea of several beats in length to serve as the motive or the "leader." Let the motive end on a strong beat with an indefinite cadence.
2) The note on which the beginning motive ends will coincide with the entrance of the imitation of this motive in the "follower"; therefore, these two points must agree.
3) Choice of the interval of imitation should be limited to the octave or the fifth. These are the most useful and the most practical intervals. Other intervals of imitation are possible, but can present great difficulties in the control of tonality and chord progression.
   a) With imitation at the octave, the problem is in obtaining some harmonic variety, and with imitation at the fifth, a feeling of modulation to the dominant should be avoided.
   b) Either voice may be the "leader." If the "leader" is the top voice, the significance of the line when it is imitated as a lower voice must be anticipated. If the "leader" is the lower voice, it must not degenerate into a bass line, but must maintain a melodic "flow."
4) After the first two entrances of the beginning motive have been set down, the "leader" is extended as *counterpoint* to the first motive, now in the "follower." This new line is then moved into the "follower" as was done with the beginning motive, and another counterpoint is written against it in the "leader." This procedure continues, always being certain that the new material added continues the "leader" as a good melodic line, and that principles of *unity* and *variety* are observed.
5) On arrival at the desired point of cadence, or ending, there are two choices:
   a) The voices may each end separately (as in a "round").
      A good feeling of melodic cadence is arrived at in the "leader" (ending on the tonic note) and the voice stops with a note of longer value. This ending is then imitated in the "follower."
   b) The voices may end together.
      The two voices may end as above, except that the "leader" continues after its cadence, reinforcing the final cadence in the "follower." In this case, if the "follower" is the upper voice, then the imitated cadence pattern may be weaker than it was before, using the added lower voice to give strength to the final cadence. If the "follower" is the lower voice, then the imitated cadence pattern may be more harmonic in character.
6) Test the lines independently, and together. Watch out for "dead" spots, where rhythmic movement may stop unexpectedly. Try to notice the harmonic progression. Be certain that there is enough harmonic change (especially if imitation is at the octave), or that there is no questionable harmonic structure or progression.

MODEL (KEYED TO INSTRUCTIONS):

MODEL 3

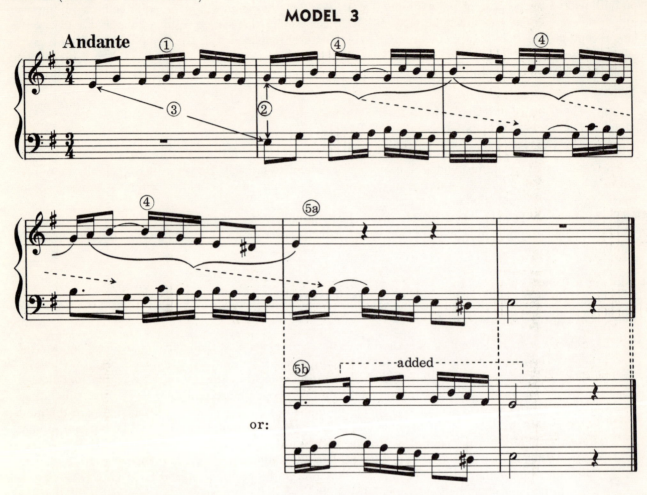

Assignment

1) Write canons in two voices, using original motives in various styles.
2) Use the interval of the octave. You may experiment with the fifth and other intervals, but carefully test the results.
3) Make each canon from five to ten measures long.

Chapter 12

Simple Contrapuntal Devices

One of the strongest characteristics of the music of Bach is the sparseness of the original material with which he builds whole, often very significant, compositions. This is achieved by the technique of "contrapuntal manipulation," in which the composer's originality and imagination allow him to use the same basic material continually, but in different ways, for constant variety. This manipulation, or "development," is achieved by the application of certain characteristic contrapuntal devices. As an example, nearly all of the melodic material of Bach's Invention 1 can be traced directly to contrapuntal manipulation of two small melodic ideas.

EXAMPLE 79A

EXAMPLE 79B

THE DEVICES

1) Canonic Development

The technique of canonic writing has been covered in Chapter 11. Its application as a means of contrapuntal manipulation will be seen in the study of the Inventions to follow.

In order for a passage to be considered really canonic, the exact imitation must be continued significantly beyond the length of the original motive. Instead of a definite ending, the canonic passage will *dissolve* into further development.

2) Sequence

This is probably the most common contrapuntal device. Its value is in spinning out a relatively short melodic idea and carrying the line forward using a minimum of material. It gives a strong feeling of unity. (For specific details, see Chapter 2, page 16)

53

Sequential figures, as indeed all figures and motives in the music of Bach, usually have the rhythmic shape of moving forward from the weaker part of a beat or measure toward, and ending on, the strong. This is one of the things which gives this music its characteristic "drive." It is always leaning *forward* toward the next beat, and carrying the listener with it.

EXAMPLE 80

W. T. C. I, Fugue II

3) Imitation

This is a type of melodic recurrence which involves at least two voices. The second voice "imitates" what the first voice has just finished.

The imitation may be in the same, but usually in a different, register. It may be on the same scale steps as the original or on different scale steps. Any interval of imitation is possible.

If all the melodic intervals of the recurrence are the same as in the original, then the imitation is said to be "strict."

a) An imitation at the octave is always "strict" (Example 81a).

b) Imitation at other intervals than the octave may be strict by nature, or, if not, they may be made to be strict by the addition of accidentals to change interval quality (Example 81b).

Strict Imitation:

EXAMPLE 81A

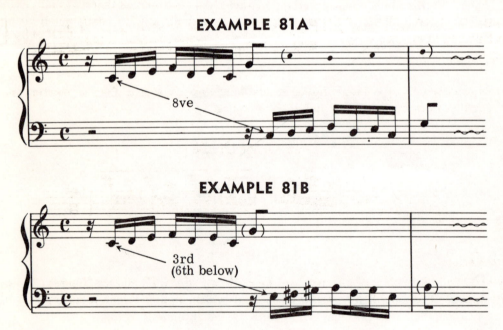

8ve

EXAMPLE 81B

3rd
(6th below)

If the size or quality of any melodic interval is changed, or is different from the corresponding interval in the original, then the imitation is said to be "free."

FREE IMITATION:

EXAMPLE 82

2nd
(7th below)

*The quality of these intervals differs from the corresponding intervals of the original.

Imitation is a very freely used device. It is the basis for the construction of the exposition, or introductory section, of an invention or a fugue, and also is useful in the development of ideas, utilizing both complete figures, or motives, or just fragmentary parts of a figure.

4) Repetition

This device is exactly what the name indicates. It is the immediate recurrence of a figure or motive in the same voice and on the same scale steps. Repetition is not commonly used because any immediate repetition within a melodic line slows or stops the forward movement of the line.

EXAMPLE 83

Invention 3

As this example shows, a longer figure is less dangerous to repeat than a shorter one would be. Short repetitions can become fussy and even annoying.

EXAMPLE 84

Invention 8

As this example shows, a longer figure is less dangerous to repeat than a shorter one would be.

5) Fragmentation

Any melodic idea of any significance will be made up of several shorter "figures." These figures are usually defined as containing from three to six tones which seem to belong together.

EXAMPLE 85

W. T. C. I, Fugue III

There are many possibilities for finding short figures, each of which may be useful as the starting point for sequential or imitative passages.

6) Inversion (Contrary Motion)

This is one of the most important of the simpler devices. Here each melodic movement is the reverse of that in the original figure or passage.

EXAMPLE 86

(Original)   (Inversion)

As can be seen, the quality of the intervals may differ from the original, depending upon the scale steps involved.

The procedure for arriving at the inversion of a figure will be as follows:

a) If the inversion is to appear within the same harmonic formation as the original figure, the 3rd of the basic chord in the original should be located. Keeping this note the same, the melodic intervals can be worked both ways from this, moving in the opposite direction from the corresponding intervals in the original figure.

EXAMPLE 87

(Original)   (Inverted)

b) Lacking an obvious chord 3rd, then the procedure would be to make tonic notes in the original figure dominant notes in the inversion, and dominant notes tonic.

EXAMPLE 88

c) To place the figure in another chord or key in the inversion, the above procedure may be followed first, and the resulting inversion simply transposed to the desired key or chord. The same results can be arrived at by inverting *directly* into the new chord or key by the following procedures:

(1) By making the third of the original key or chord the third of the new key or chord, or

(2) By making the tonic note of the original key or chord the dominant note of the new key or chord, and the dominant of the original the tonic of the new.

(3) The addition of accidentals is a specific problem of each inversion and will follow obvious principles and requirements of chord and key.

EXAMPLE 89A

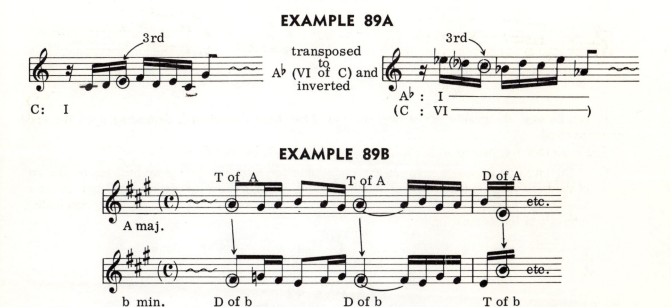

EXAMPLE 89B

An inversion may be used as an immediate recurrence as in an imitation, or may appear during development anywhere.

7) Combination of Devices

Various combinations of some of the above devices are very commonly used. An illustration is the sequence of the inversion of the motive in Invention 1 (measures 3 and 4, upper voice), and in the same Invention, measure 6, first and second beats, upper voice, there is a fragmentation of the inverted motive which is used in sequence. These should be examined carefully. Such manipulations are very common. This is the "meat" of contrapuntal writing, the possibilities limited only by the limitations of the composer's imagination.

8) Other Devices

There are several other possibilities for the manipulation of material, but none are as frequent nor as useful as the above.

a) The *size* of an interval (or several intervals) may be changed in an imitation or statement. This refers to the actual numerical designation of the interval, as "2nd," "3rd," "4th," and so forth.

EXAMPLE 90

Original

*size of interval changed

b) The *quality* of one or more intervals may be changed. This refers to the major, minor, augmented, or diminished designation of an interval. This occurs commonly in sequence patterns, and also produces the change of mode of a figure or motive between major and minor.

EXAMPLE 91

*quality of interval changed

c) Notes may be added (interpolated) around, or within, the notes of a motive or figure.

EXAMPLE 92

*elaborated

The only restriction in the use of these possible manipulations is that the changes do not distort the original shape and character of the line beyond recognition.

Study Questions

1) How is canonic writing used as a means of development?
2) What is the value of sequence?
3) Where is imitation found most commonly?
4) How is imitation used as development?
5) What is repetition, and what are its values and limitations?
6) What is fragmentation?
7) Find figures that would be useful for development in several Bach motives.
8) What is inversion?
9) What is the procedure for arriving at an inversion?
10) Describe and illustrate possible combinations of devices.
11) What are other ways of developing a melodic idea?

Exercises in the Manipulation of Given Motives

1) Write illustrations of the various devices of manipulation using the following motives.
2) It will be found that not all motives will work equally well with all devices.
3) The final note of each motive is of indefinite value because this will depend upon the possible continuation of this line.

EXERCISE 13

Chapter 13

Natural Double (Invertible) Counterpoint

Natural Double Counterpoint, sometimes called Invertible Counterpoint, is a process whereby two voices are written in such a way that either voice may be used above or below the other without encountering unpleasant or technically questionable interval relationships. This means that each of the original lines must be a good melodic line in itself. Undesirable intervals must be anticipated as the original version is written.

1) The interval of a fifth between the voices is possible, although weak in prominent rhythmic positions, but when voices are rearranged this interval becomes a usually undesirable fourth. From this it can be seen that fifths should be avoided in prominent position if the voices are intended to be used in inverted form.

2) The location of the questionable interval rhythmically is important in deciding its possible use. If it appears as a definite non-chord tone, then it may be possible that even dissonant intervals may be harmless.

3) This danger occurs with all classes of intervals except the *primary consonances*. Best results are obtained when essential intervals are mostly thirds and sixths. (An occasional octave is possible, subject to the usual conditions for this interval.)

The two versions of the pair of voices may follow each other immediately,

EXAMPLE 93

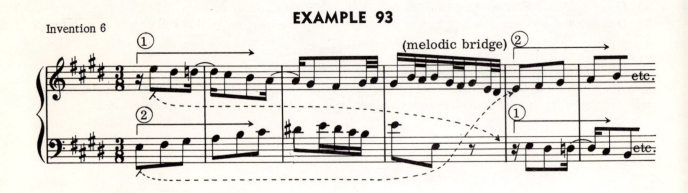

Or, the inverted version may appear later in the piece in another section, and often in another key from the original.

1) In this case, the inversion into the new key is made by keeping the tonic note (or the root of the chord) of the original version as the tonic (or root) of the new key (or chord), but placing it in the other voice.
2) Note that the sum of the distances that each voice has moved is an octave. The lower voice of the original has moved *up* a second (plus an octave), and the upper voice of the original has moved *down* a seventh. The addition of an octave to either or both of these movements has nothing to do with the basic movements, but only places the voices in the desired range and relationship without letting them cross each other. This octave relationship will always exist in Natural Double Counterpoint.

Study Questions

1) What is Natural Double Counterpoint?
2) What are the general problems?
3) How is it useful?
4) Describe the process of interchanging two lines to remain in the same key.
5) Describe the process of interchanging two lines so that the inverted version will appear in a different key.

Exercises in Natural Double Counterpoint

Write numerous two-voice examples according to the principles of Natural Double Counterpoint and interchange them to appear in the same key, and in other keys, adding accidentals as necessary.

*. . . good contrapuntal construc-
tions demand something more
than the mere emotional fancy
of a naive composer. . . .*
—PAUL HINDEMITH

Part II

INTRODUCTION

Polyphonic music falls into certain conventional patterns — canonic, fugal, or developmental. All of these contain elements of the others, but have certain characteristics peculiar to themselves. Most of the polyphonic music of Bach, and of this period, can be placed in one of these three categories:

1) The *Canon* is strictly imitative throughout, as has been seen. It is the most strict and exacting of the three.

2) The *Fugue* has certain strict characteristics peculiar to it, but can be much more expressive because of the added element of freedom in its developmental sections.

3) The *Invention* is the least strict of the three and probably the easiest to write. It is imitative and developmental.

Bach's two-voice Inventions were written, as a preface to one of his manuscripts states, as studies in style for his students in which they might learn how best to develop melodic ideas, and to "form" a piece of music. It must be realized that any keyboard player was expected to improvise, and these were examples to keyboard students (and to composers) of the best ways of developing and extending melodic ideas into well-rounded pieces of music in a two-voice texture.

For today's student, they serve as a concise lexicon of the contrapuntal practices of Bach, and of the musicians of the time. What happens in these pieces is peculiar not only to keyboard music, but is basic to all of the music in this style, no matter what the medium. In the Inventions, these practices appear in an easily obtainable form where they may be studied and emulated.

The ramifications of these studies must not be overlooked. These are not the "antiquated" practices of a dead era, but are alive today in the practices of innumerable contemporary composers. Only the idiom has changed.

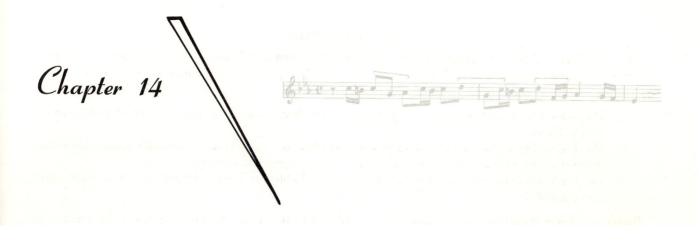

Chapter 14

The Two-Voice Invention – A

The factors for consideration in the study of the Inventions are:

1) The Motive
2) The Counterpoint, or Countermotive
3) The Exposition
4) The Episodes
5) The Form

THE MOTIVE

In general, a motive is a short melodic idea made up of several figures (Chapter 12, page 55), ending with an indefinite cadence. Specifically, a motive is the "theme" of the invention.

1) The motive should have some striking characteristic, melodic or rhythmic, which will make it easily recognizable each time it is heard.

EXAMPLE 95A

Contrast of
Melodic Movement

EXAMPLE 95B

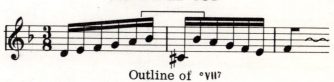

Outline of °VII⁷

2) It should lend itself to contrapuntal manipulation.
3) It will be harmonically simple and regular, often implying only one chord.

EXAMPLE 96

e min.: I

4) The first note or notes should give an unmistakable tonic impression.
5) Its range should not exceed an octave and is usually less.
6) It will usually be at least two beats long. In the simpler inventions it will seldom exceed six beats.

EXAMPLE 97

C: I

a) The three-eight time which Bach occasionally uses is treated as a compound single beat per measure.

EXAMPLE 98

7) There are other types of inventions which have motives varying from the above characteristics, to be discussed later. (See Chapter 17.)

THE COUNTERMOTIVE, OR THE COUNTERPOINT

In an invention, the first occurrence following the initial statement of the motive is an imitation of the motive in the other of the two voices. As this occurs, the first voice continues with a line written as a counterpoint to the motive as it appears in the second voice.

1) This line should be a smooth continuation of the statement of the motive in the first voice.
2) It will reinforce the motive, rhythmically and harmonically, and add any necessary clarification or contrast to the motive line as it appears in the second voice in imitation.

EXAMPLE 99

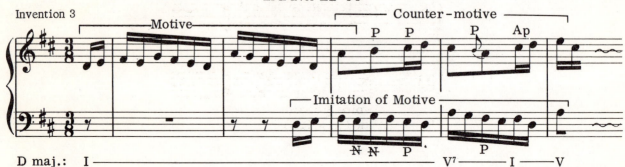

D maj.:   I

Countermotive: Clarifies strong beats after pick-up
Reinforces harmony
Provides rhythmic contrast to motive

If, on further examination, the counterpoint line is found to be used rather consistently, either with the motive or developed independently, in later parts of the invention, then it is a true *countermotive*.

If this line is insignificant and does not appear again in easily recognizable form, then it will be termed simply the *counterpoint*.

THE EXPOSITION

The first recognizable unit of form in an invention is the *exposition*. Its function is to present the material which is going to become the basis for the evolution of the rest of the invention.

In the two-voice invention, the exposition will be composed of:

1) Statements of the motive
2) Imitations of the motive
3) The countermotive (or counterpoint)

The exposition will begin and end within the principal key, usually on the tonic at both points.

1) Sometimes the exposition may close with the dominant chord (semicadence).
2) Rarely will any but chords of tonic or dominant classification appear in the exposition.

The motive is usually announced alone in the upper voice.

1) If the beginning notes of the motive do not firmly establish the tonic, then a few notes may be added in the other voice as accompaniment.

EXAMPLE 100

2) If the tonic is well defined by the motive, there is no need for a second voice at this point.
3) Sometimes an accompanying voice may be needed to clarify or reinforce the rhythm of the motive in addition to adding harmonic strength.

EXAMPLE 101

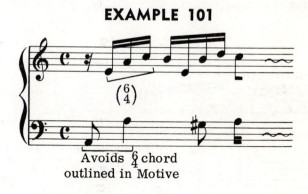

Avoids $\frac{6}{4}$ chord
outlined in Motive

The lower voice then imitates the first statement of the motive. This imitation is usually at the octave, although the fifth (fourth below) is sometimes used.

The upper voice, which first announced the motive, now continues with the countermotive or counterpoint.

EXAMPLE 102A

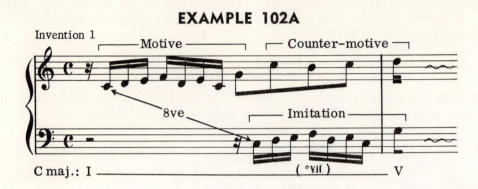

EXAMPLE 102B

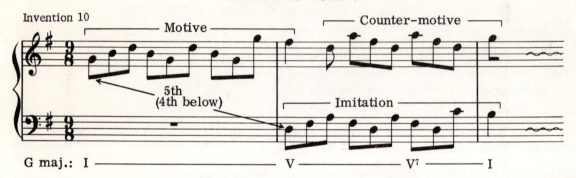

There are three basic patterns for the structure of the exposition of a two-voice invention. The following diagrams of those patterns show motive (M), countermotive (CM), accompanying voice (/////), and intervals of each imitation from the original statement.

1) THE TWO-ENTRANCE EXPOSITION:

a)

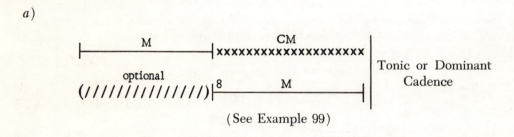

b)

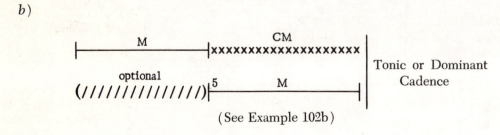

Occasionally in any exposition, the last interval of the last entrance may be changed to produce a stronger cadence.

2) THE THREE-ENTRANCE EXPOSITION:

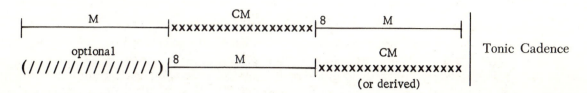

EXAMPLE 103

The third entrance, again in the upper voice, will be in a different (higher) register than the original announcement, although on the same scale steps. This exposition will work well only in certain keys and with motives of rather limited range because of the problem of tessitura (range of voices).

3) THE FOUR-ENTRANCE EXPOSITION:

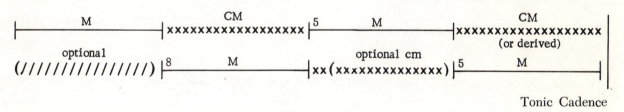

EXAMPLE 104

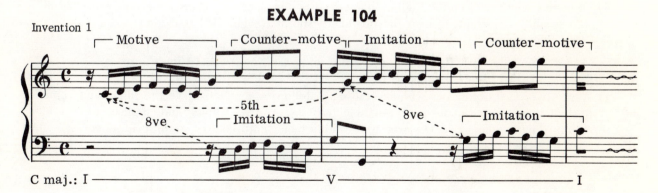

This exposition is so perfect in balance and function as to be termed "classic," although it is not as common as the term would suggest. It divides itself into two parts, usually very parallel with each other, one tonic and the other dominant. Often freedom is taken with the fourth entrance so that the exposition will end on the tonic chord. (See Example 104.) It is most effective with a short concise motive.

The structure of the motive is found to have an influence on the type of exposition which can be used.

1) A motive which ends on the tonic note (root of the tonic chord) can only be followed by a tonic imitation, so such a motive will require the use of either the three-entrance, or two-entrance exposition. (See Invention 8 with a two-entrance exposition.)

2) A motive which ends on the mediant of the scale (third of the tonic chord) can only be followed by a tonic imitation, and must be handled with either a three- or two-entrance exposition. (See Invention 4 with a three-entrance exposition.)

3) A motive which ends on the dominant note is the most flexible because this note can be used either as the fifth of the tonic chord, allowing a tonic imitation to follow, or as the root of the dominant chord, allowing the imitation to be dominant. This motive lends itself equally well to either the two-entrance or the four-entrance exposition. Length of the motive should be the governing factor in choice of the type of exposition in this case. (See Invention 1 with a four-entrance exposition, and Invention 3 with a two-entrance exposition.)

When the dominant note as the last note of the motive is approached by leap (usually from the tonic), it can be used in either connotation equally well. Another advantage of ending a motive in this way is that the leap can be altered (i.e., a fifth changed to a fourth) in the last entrance in the exposition to allow the exposition to end on the tonic chord.

EXAMPLE 105

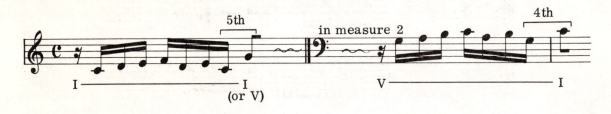

If the dominant note is approached by step, dominant harmony is much more strongly implied, and would require the two-entrance (tonic-dominant) exposition to be used in most cases. This is uncommon.

4) A motive which ends on the leading tone (third of the dominant chord), or very exceptionally on the second scale step (fifth of the dominant chord), could be used only in a two-entrance (tonic-dominant) exposition.

Exercises

1) Write two-voice expositions with several of the following motives. Make the expositions complete, including imitations in the most workable patterns, countermotive, and if necessary, optional accompanying voice. End the exposition with a tonic chord (on the strong beat, of course) whenever possible.

MOTIVES:

EXERCISE 14

2) Write original motives in varied keys and styles, and use several as the basis for two-voice expositions.

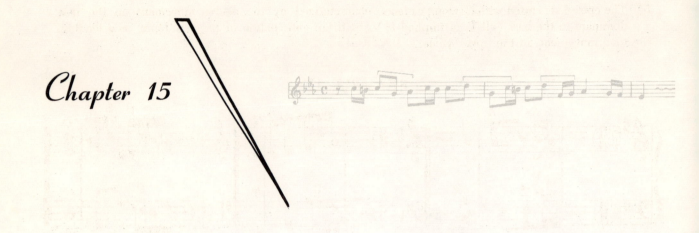

Chapter 15

The Two-Voice Invention—B

The *episodes* of the invention are those parts of the form in which creative originality is most evident. At the completion of the exposition, the harmony is usually tonic. The chord which serves as the end of the exposition (on a strong beat) will also serve as the first chord of the episode which follows. The technique of thus tying the two together is called "elision."

EXAMPLE 106

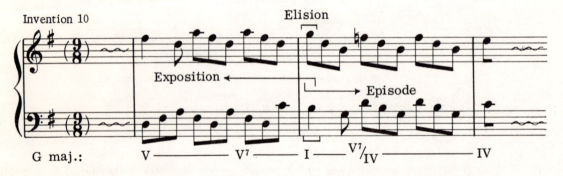

An episode is a development passage in free form, usually modulatory.

1) The motive and the countermotive are "manipulated," or developed, by various devices according to the originality and technique of the composer. (See Chapter 12.)

2) The material of the episode is said to be "derived" from the elements of the exposition. It is possible for a few measures of the first episode to be written as natural double counterpoint for later use. (See Chapter 13.)

3) The first episode should be a smooth, natural continuation of the exposition. It may be begun by substituting the devices of *sequence, inversion,* or *repetition* for the imitative devices characteristic of the exposition, or tasteful combinations of these devices.

4) More harmonic variety will appear in the episode, often partially governed by sequence patterns. The episode will usually modulate to and end with a cadence in a next-related key.

5) The episode is ended with a strong cadence, characterized by the octave movement on the new dominant in the bass (all V, or implied I_4^6 V) with an anticipation of the new tonic, or a leading-tone movement, in the upper voice.

EXAMPLE 107

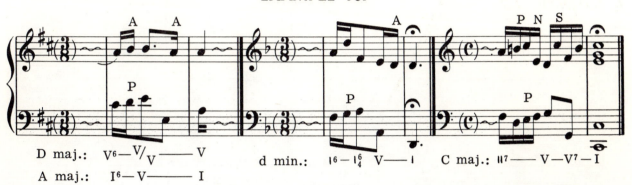

D maj.: V^6 — V/V ——— V

A maj.: I^6 — V ——— I

d min.: I^6 — I_4^6 V —— I

C maj.: II^7 —— V — V^7 — I

Method of Analysis

1) A system of symbols will denote thematic relationships:

   a) ⊢————————⊣ — Motive in exposition (or any clearly defined statement of the motive). Use number of scale step at beginning of symbol to show where it starts.

   b) xxxxxxxxxxxxxxxxxx — Countermotive or counterpoint.

   c) ///////////////// — Accompanying figure (in exposition only).

   d) — — — — — — — — — Episodic material derived from the motive.

   (1) <u>inv.</u> _ _ _ _ _ — By inversion.

   e) oooooooooooooooo — Episodic material derived from the countermotive.

   f) — — — ⌐ — — — ⌐ — Sequence indicated by brackets over symbol denoting derivation. Bracket to cover amount of material in sequence.

   g) ～～～～～～～～ — Free material (not obviously derived).

   h) Pp5 ～～～～～～ — Pedal point. Number indicates scale step used as pedal point.

   i) If there is thematic material used which cannot be traced to the exposition, yet is important enough to be accounted for other than as free material, this symbol may be used:)))))))))))).

   j) Indicate rests as they occur.

2) Draw guide lines on plain paper to represent voices.
3) Draw bar lines across the guide lines to represent measure bars, and number the measures.
4) Place thematic symbols on guide lines in proper relative positions according to the bar lines and voices in which they appear.
5) Place harmonic symbols under diagram.

EXAMPLE 108

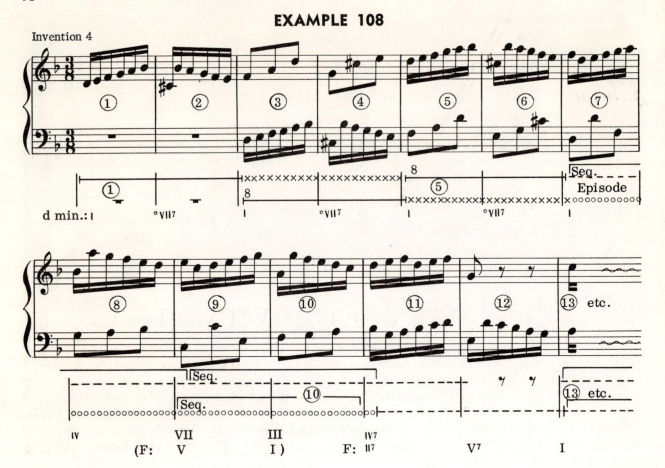

Analysis

Analyze the expositions and the following episodes (through the first strong cadence) of these Inventions: 1, 3, 7.

1) Use symbols to indicate thematic relationships.
2) Use traditional chord symbols to indicate basic harmonic progression and modulation. It is not necessary to indicate every possible harmonic combination but only the essential outline, as in Example 108.

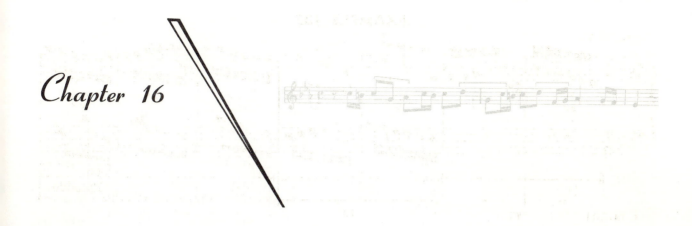

Chapter 16

The Two-Voice Invention — C

The form of the invention is usually sectional, each section supplying harmonic contrast by being in a new (next-related) key to the original tonic.

A section will be modulatory in character, progressing to the key of the next section, and attached to it by an elision (the last chord of one section serving as the first of the next section). Each section will be defined by a very strong cadence. This cadence is stylized in the music of Bach and the expected form should be used. (See Chapter 15, page 73) Cadence material may be free (not derived) since harmonic progression is the important element here.

THE FIRST SECTION

The first section of an invention is made up of the exposition and the first episode, the episode being a few measures longer than the exposition. How much longer it will be will depend somewhat on the devices of manipulation used. First sections will be approximately the same, regardless of the overall form of the invention.

EXAMPLE 109

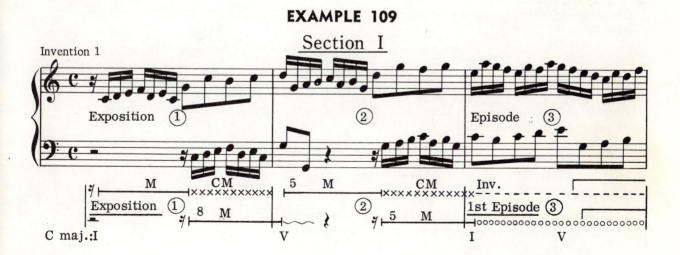

THE COUNTEREXPOSITION

Occasionally an invention will contain a *counterexposition* at the beginning of the second section. The purpose of this counterexposition is to provide a balance with the original exposition. It will be of similar construction to the original exposition except that:

1) The thematic material will appear in opposite voices.
2) It will be in a contrasting key.
3) It is often shorter (never longer) than the original exposition.

Its use is optional and is not found excessively in the music being studied. The example which follows should be compared to the original measures in Invention 1 in order to see the context in which they appear.

EXAMPLE 110

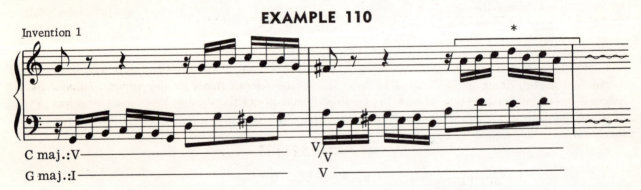

*This imitation is a fourth lower than it should be to correspond with the pattern. The counterexposition ends on the third beat. Compare with measures 1 and 2 of Example 109.

The counterexposition here is one entrance shorter than the exposition. The apparent fourth entrance of the motive is on the wrong scale steps to fit the pattern of the exposition, so must be considered to be part of the second episode.

THE REMAINING SECTIONS

The differences in the Inventions of Bach begin to appear at this point. An Invention may contain two or three sections.

1) They are related to each other by common material.
2) They contrast in key (at least at the beginning).
3) They will approximately balance each other in length.

Occasionally a section may have a rather strong cadence near the middle which will have the effect of dividing it into "subsections." Common devices, or other common characteristics will, however, prevent the impression that there are two independent sections. (See Invention 3. The second section extends from measure 12 through measure 42, with a cadence into measure 24. Also see Chapter 17, page 81, in reference to this Invention.)

Definite key plans are characteristic of these sectional forms.

1) THE THREE-SECTION INVENTION:

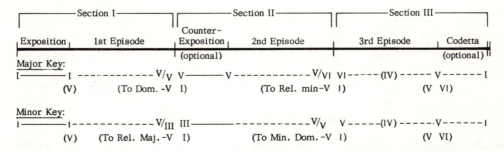

2) THE TWO-SECTION INVENTION:

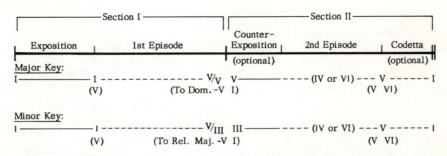

In the **three-section invention**, the harmonic contrasts are obtained by going to the *dominant* or *relative major* for the beginning of the second section, and to the *relative minor* or the *minor dominant* for the beginning of the third section, depending upon the modality of the starting key (major or minor).

EXAMPLE 111

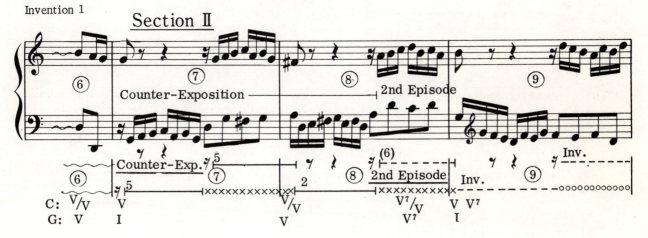

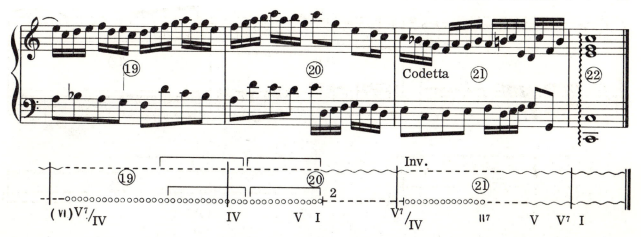

(Note that there is no counterexposition in the third section, measure 15, Example 111.)

A codetta is optional in this or any form. When used, it will usually follow a deceptive cadence, and will reiterate the cadence pattern to the tonic. (See Invention 3, measure 54 to end.)

Sometimes a cadence to the minor subdominant is substituted for the cadence to the minor dominant for the third section in a minor key. The *minor* dominant is used because it represents a next-related key to the original tonic whereas the *major* dominant, as a key, would not.

In the **two-section invention**, there may be more harmonic contrast in the middle of the second section than is indicated in the diagram, almost to the point of subdividing the section. (See Invention 8, Section 2, measure 12 to end, and Invention 10, Section 2, measure 14 to end.)

In overall length, there is little difference in this and in the three-section form, indicating that the sections are apt to be longer in the two-section form. Sometimes Section 2 will overbalance Section 1 in length. (See Invention 8.)

The tonalities shown for each of the sections will not last for the whole section. Usually a few chords will be enough to provide the desired contrast, and then a return to the original tonic, or an unsettled modulatory (usually sequential) progression can be expected.

Analysis

Analyze the following Inventions thematically and harmonically by chart, indicating sections as they occur:

    1) Three-section — Inventions 4 and 7
    2) Two-section — Inventions 8 and 10

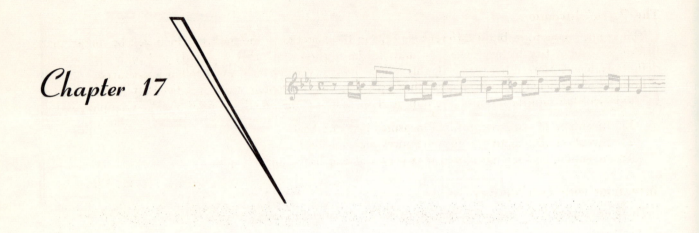

Chapter 17

The Two-Voice Invention – D

Inventions in other forms than the sectional form already discussed are frequent. The most common examples need to be examined.

Inventions in Song Form

1) The **three-part song form** is found on occasion in the Inventions. The characteristic of this form is a return to the beginning, both in key and in thematic presentation for the third section. The return need not be carried out for long, but enough of the beginning must be heard again to give a definite impression of return. This is sometimes referred to as an A B A form. As examples, see Invention 3 with its return to the beginning in measure 43, and Invention 6 in which the return, in measure 43, has the voices interchanged.

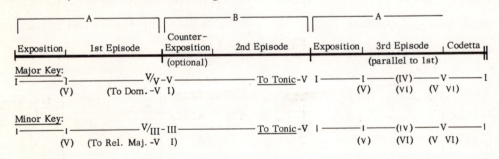

The third episode may begin like the first episode, but then will probably become more independent in order to remain in the tonic and establish the original key firmly.

2) The **two-part song form** is so much like the two-section form already described that most music resembling this (at least, in this style) can be called sectional.

3) Another variant is that of an invention which is built up of a group of short sections, each with a statement of the motive, usually in different keys, followed by a short development of about the same length as the motive.

There will be a smoothly outlined key plan with each section providing varying degrees of harmonic contrast. This type is usually found in inventions with long motives. As an example, see Invention 14 in which the motive is three measures and one beat in length.

The "Lyric" Invention

This is not a new form but a different concept in the material of the motive, which will be longer than before, sometimes two to four measures, and will be a phrase (possibly a period) in length with a more definite cadence. More often than not, this motive will be accompanied in its initial appearance.

Because of the length of the motive, the exposition will not contain more than two entrances, and often this type will fall into the form of a group of short sections, described on page 80. As examples, see:

1) Invention 14 — motive is three measures and one beat
2) Invention 15 — motive is two measures and one beat
3) Invention 11 — motive is two measures and one beat (upper voice)

Inventions with Two Motives

There are three typical ways in which to construct an invention using two motives.

1) A new motive may be used as the basis for a section (usually the second section).

The new motive will be a derivation of, or closely related to, the original motive, and will appear only in one section, with a return to the original motive in the next.

EXAMPLE 112

Sometimes the new motive will appear again, or be alluded to, in the codetta.

EXAMPLE 113

Here, as in all cases where two motives are used in an invention, the first motive will be designated as Motive A and the second as Motive B. In an analysis by diagram, these letters should be used with the symbols denoting the use of the motive, whether a statement or a derivation, during episodes.

2) Two motives may appear at the beginning of the invention, each with its own separate exposition. Usually the development of these motives will be alternated in episodic sections. These motives will have a close similarity, but will be definitely separate.

EXAMPLE 114

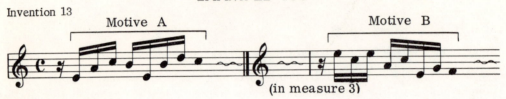

In this type, the second motive has a tendency to be much less important than the first. These motives are often "lyric" in character.

3) Two motives may appear simultaneously in the exposition.

EXAMPLE 115

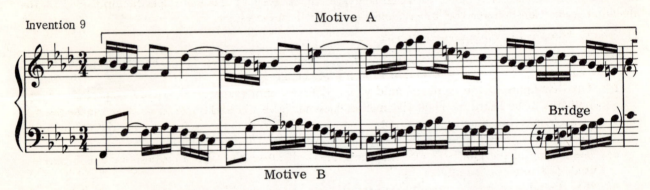

This is probably the most common type of the use of two motives. These two voices are real "contrapuntal associates." They are conceived together, and generally stay together, even in derived episodic passages, although they may also be developed separately.

It is expected that they will be written in natural double counterpoint, so that their relationship may be interchanged. Sometimes they are very similar in character, or they may be contrasting.

There should be no confusion between this and a motive with accompanying voice. These will be much more important and will be used consistently throughout. (Compare Invention 15 and Invention 9. See Inventions 6, 11, and 12, all having two motives.)

It is possible that elements of different styles may be combined so that the above types may overlap and be more than just one kind of invention.

Analysis
Analyze fully by chart the Inventions quoted as examples of the various types in the text: Inventions 3, 6, 9, 11, 12, 13, 14, 15.

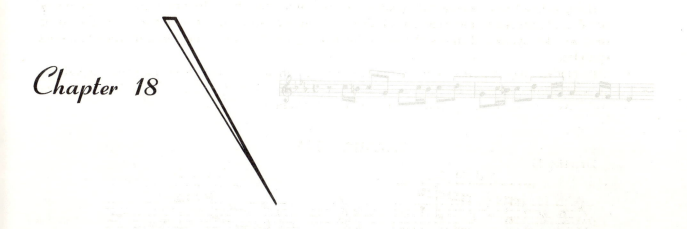

Chapter 18

Writing a Two-Voice Invention

In writing a two-voice invention, it will be necessary to keep in mind all that has gone before concerning the basic elements of melody and two-voice counterpoint, as well as the more specific principles of the invention itself. Constant referral to previous chapters will be necessary.

1) The first step is to decide upon a motive.

   a) Since there are several varieties of two-voice inventions, some thought needs to be given to the choice of the form of the invention as it will affect the motive.

   b) The first figure of the motive should give a definite impression of the tonic, especially if the motive is to be heard alone. If the motive does not have the tonic note at or near the beginning, an accompanying line, or a few notes, may be added in the other voice to make the tonic feeling more definite. (Chapter 14, page 67.)

   c) The ending of the motive is also important and will affect the type of exposition which may be used. (Chapter 14, page 70.)

   d) It is desirable to try a motive in an exposition to see what will happen as to range and harmonic continuity before deciding upon it.

2) The countermotive is also worthy of considerable thought and experimentation.

   a) Remember that this line must complement the motive to help reinforce harmonic implications. It also can be used to smooth out any possible rhythmic gaps in the motive.

   b) It can be very helpful in supplying additional thematic material for later episodic use if it can be made characteristic and independent enough.

3) In writing the exposition, these points should be remembered:

   a) The countermotive should be a smooth and natural continuation of the motive.

   b) The harmonic content should be kept simple and logical (tonic and dominant, for the most part). Beware of incidental implied harmonies that may complicate the harmonic progression if they are too strong.

   c) Avoid complexity. Remember that there is a whole invention ahead. Added movement may be needed later on to maintain interest. The purpose of the exposition is to present the material. The episodes are the places for freedom and movement.

4) The episodes need to be planned. Generally, the most simple manipulations will occur first, the more complex later. It is a good idea to decide mentally upon a distribution of devices of development so that each episode will have something fresh and new to present.

a) Keep in mind the possibilities of natural double counterpoint in the first episode to be used later in another section. Try to make the two lines interesting and the result worthy of using again.

b) It is advisable to spend some time experimenting with the motive and the countermotive, writing short excerpts of development from which to choose material and ideas to use in the episodes.

c) The first episode will be a few measures longer than the exposition. The others will approximately balance this in length.

5) If a counterexposition is desired, this needs to be written before the ending of the first episode so that it can be seen where the voices must be led to give a smooth elision.

6) A codetta may be added to the last section. This can be two to four measures in length. It is very successful to use a deceptive cadence into the codetta. (See Invention 3, last six measures, and Invention 4, last four measures.) The main functions of a codetta will be to reiterate the tonic cadence and possibly to give a last statement of the motive.

One thing to remember: Bach is the teacher, and most questions that will arise can be answered in his two-voice Inventions. Constant referral to them is desirable, advised, and encouraged.

Assignment

Write Inventions as assigned.

He should be called not Bach
['*brook*'] *but* Mer ['*sea*'] *on ac-
count of his endlessly inexhaust-
ible wealth of musical ideas.*
—Beethoven

Part III

Chapter 19

The Association of Three Voices

Three-voice counterpoint is undoubtedly the most gratifying texture with which to work. The three voices allow the use of more complete harmonic structures, giving an opportunity for maximum harmonic strength. The three voices also allow for more rhythmic and melodic variety without overloading any one voice. There is space to move the voices comfortably without exceeding ranges, yet the texture allows for contrasts in range and color through close and widespread groupings.

This increased harmonic strength can be dangerous, however, if it is allowed to become more prominent than the melodic and rhythmic movement of the voices. A horizontal feeling must still be maintained in spite of the increased implications of the vertical coincidence of tones.

MELODIC MOVEMENT

The individual melodic lines in a three-voice texture are governed by the same principles as before. (Chapter 2, page 11.) Because of the richer harmonic texture, it is necessary that the melodic lines be strong, and conceal rather than reinforce harmonic implications in many instances. (Chapter 2, page 16.)

1) Arpeggiation should be used cautiously because of its inherent harmonic implication. (Chapter 2, page 11.)
2) The stronger non-chord tones (accented passing tones, accented auxiliaries, suspensions, and appoggiaturas) are most useful in weakening harmonic implications through delay of, and substitution for, the principal melodic tones.
3) The neighboring tone and escape tone can be used more successfully in three voices, the other two voices being used to make the desired harmony more definite. (Chapter 1, page 9.)

The tie becomes more common and is very valuable in providing melodic independence. (Chapter 1, page 6.) Ties and syncopations which might have been considered exceptional in two voices are now possible. The movement of the other voices can be used to make the rhythmic pulse more definite.

EXAMPLE 116A

EXAMPLE 116B

It is not recommended that two voices be tied at the same time, but it is possible if the third voice maintains the rhythmic movement strongly enough.

EXAMPLE 117

Repeated notes can be found more frequently than in two voices, but usually as a characteristic feature of a thematic figure.

EXAMPLE 118A

EXAMPLE 118B

EXAMPLE 118C

This device is an artistic one and must be justified — a difficult task sometimes.

The pedal point is frequent in any voice, although most common in the bass.

EXAMPLE 119

*B♭ pedal point not part of chord

A pedal point must begin and end as a chord tone, but need not be part of every chord for its entire duration. Occasionally a pedal point may be left as a well resolved suspension.

RHYTHMIC MOVEMENT

As in two voices, the rhythmic activity needs to be equally divided between the voices to provide balance.

As a rhythmic element, the tie should be mentioned here again, its value being to provide rhythmic independence to a line. A repeated warning, however, is that the normal pulse must be well defined in another voice.

Often the same rhythmic pattern may be found in two voices at the same time, with the third voice providing contrast.

EXAMPLE 120

1) This should not be continued for more than a few beats between the same pair of voices. Any extended use of this is more frequent in four-voice counterpoint.

2) It is frequent that voices moving in parallel rhythmic movement also will be in parallel thirds or sixths, but again, only for a few beats at a time.

EXAMPLE 121

3) In three-voice texture, it is possible for one voice to carry all, or most, of the rhythmic activity for a rather extended time if the other two voices maintain a necessary amount of interest. The danger here is in allowing the other two voices to degenerate into "accompaniment."

EXAMPLE 122

(upper voices imitative)

Rests are much more useful and necessary in three-voice texture. They "ventilate" the texture and provide a valuable means of obtaining contrast. (Chapter 1, page 6.)

1) **Short rests,** such as eighth or sixteenth (or sometimes quarter in alla breve), are still used as they were in two voices. This can be described as emphasis of an entrance of a thematic idea by slight delay. The unexpected entrance of a voice with a new idea on a weak part of a beat after a short rest draws the listener's attention to this voice.

EXAMPLE 123

W. T. C. I, Fugue II

2) **Longer rests** of several beats, or sometimes a measure or two, will occur in only one voice at a time. Their usefulness is twofold:

   a) They supply relief and contrast from a constant three-voice texture if it begins to become monotonous or too heavy (see Fugue XV, measures 73 through 76), or they may be used to emphasize strongly a statement of thematic material when the voice so omitted returns.

   b) The voice which is to contain such a rest will stop on an inactive scale step or a tone with no tendency to fulfill, often the root of the momentary chord, and on a strong beat or fraction. Within the individual voice the effect is of temporary cadence. The following are only a few of the examples worthy of note:

   Fugue III — measure 14, middle voice, first beat
   Fugue VI — measure 21, middle voice, first beat
   Fugue VII — measure 15, middle voice, third beat
   measure 17, lower voice, third beat
   Fugue VIII — measure 43, lower voice, first beat

   c) After a longer rest, the voice will usually return with thematic material, or at least with material of some significance, and will enter on a weak beat or fraction. Following through on the above references:

   Fugue III — middle voice re-enters, measure 16, last half of second beat with significant episodic material.
   Fugue VI — middle voice re-enters, measure 25, last half of first beat with beginning of subject inverted.
   Fugue VII — middle voice re-enters, measure 17, third beat with response version of subject in c minor.
   — lower voice re-enters, measure 20, third beat with subject in c minor.
   Fugue VIII — lower voice re-enters, measure 44, third beat with inversion of subject.

HARMONIC CONTENT

As has been pointed out, a three-voice contrapuntal texture is naturally strongly harmonic. Chordal structure is more easily determined, and the "implication" found in only two voices is now "defined" by the third voice.

It has been said in this Chapter under "Melodic Movement," that arpeggiated figures are usually avoided. However, passages such as are found throughout Fugue VII (N.B.) are not infrequent. In this case, it is thematic, both in the character of the subject and in the melodic bridge following the first statement.

The three-voice texture tends to make the lower voice sound more like a "bass line" unless care is taken. It is often that the bass, being a heavier voice by nature, may tend to move more slowly than the others, but it also must have its share in the thematic development.

Because of added harmonic strength, the use of the six-four chord must be most carefully observed and controlled. The familiar rules of traditional harmony will suffice.

1) Leaping to or from the fifth of the momentary chord in the bass should be avoided except:

   a) during repetition of the same chord,

   b) when moving into a tonic six-four joined to a dominant as a cadential six-four.

2) The use of six-four chords (real or implied) in succession must be avoided.

It is possible, because of the increased definition of chords, that slightly more advanced harmonies may be found and more easily accepted, but still the basic vocabulary of diatonic traditional harmony should prevail.

Study Questions

1) What are the main differences between three-voice and two-voice counterpoint?
2) What problem presents itself in three-voice counterpoint?
3) How is this problem overcome?
4) Review the non-chord tones and their uses.
5) What is the function of tied notes?
6) How has the use of tied notes been expanded in three-voice counterpoint?
7) When are repeated notes possible?
8) Discuss the pedal point.
9) What are the restrictions on parallel rhythmic movement?
10) What is the value in the use of rests?
11) Discuss the use and value of the short rest.
12) Discuss the use and value of longer rests.
13) How should a voice be stopped before a longer rest?
14) What is the harmonic characteristic of three-voice counterpoint?
15) What special attention needs to be paid to the bass line?

Harmonic Analysis

1) Analyze the following excerpts harmonically.
2) As in two-voice texture, determine only the basic harmonic background.
3) As an adjunct to harmonic analysis, it is necessary to determine non-chord tones. Mark these also.
4) Some may be better analyzed in a key other than the original.

Excerpts for Analysis

1) Sinfonia 1 — measure 2 through first beat of measure 7
2) Sinfonia 1 — last four measures
3) Sinfonia 3 — measure 21, third beat to end
4) Sinfonia 4 — measure 4 through third beat of measure 8
5) Sinfonia 7 — last eight measures
6) Sinfonia 9 — measure 3 through first beat of measure 5
7) Sinfonia 11 — measure 57 through first beat of measure 65
8) Fugue II — last seven measures
9) Fugue VI — measure 6 through first beat of measure 13
10) Fugue VI — measure 35 through first beat of measure 39
11) Fugue VII — third beat of measure 30 to end
12) Fugue VIII — last eleven measures (note codetta)
13) Fugue XI — measure 9 through first beat of measure 18
14) Fugue XV — last five measures
15) Fugue XXI — measure 22 through first beat of measure 30

Chapter 20

Three-Voice Writing – A

In writing three-voice counterpoint, several approaches are possible. In all, certain aims must be kept in mind.

1) The implied harmonic progression must be natural and proper.
2) A consistent style, or character, must exist between all the voices. One important means to this end is the use of imitative (or quasi-imitative) lines or figures moving from one voice to another, sometimes between two of the voices, and sometimes all three.

EXAMPLE 124

3) Also necessary is a uniform rhythmic movement. The "total rhythm" — the "sum" of the rhythmic movement in all three voices — will add up to rather consistent eighth- or sixteenth-note movement (eighth or quarter in alla breve), without "dead spots" (except possibly on occasional strong parts of beats), with no voice overloaded.

EXAMPLE 125

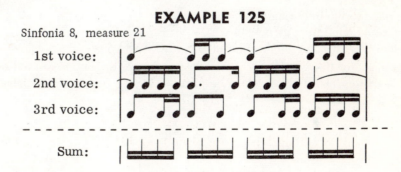

Occasional breaks from this "total rhythm" may be found in order to avoid monotony, but this steady pulse is one of the characteristics of Bach's music which gives it its inherent "drive."

4) Melodic movement should not simply "elaborate" the harmony, but must give clear, individual lines moving through harmonic reference points.

a) Adroit use of non-chord tones to conceal the harmony is necessary. Overloading lines with non-chord tones, however, can be very confusing to the ear.

b) Contrary motion is still to be considered of high value, but it is likely that two of the lines may move in parallel thirds and sixths for several beats if the other voice moves in contrary motion.

c) A voice may remain stationary in the manner of a pedal point with the other two moving in either parallel or contrary motion.

d) The balance of melodic movement between the voices should not be maintained for too long a time without change, or one may encounter monotony or loss of independence of one of the voices.

e) The middle voice should remain within an octave of one or the other of the outside voices at all times.

A common way to approach three-voice writing is by the addition of a third voice to an existing two-voice texture.

1) The two-voice material will be written according to the principles of two-voice counterpoint.

2) The third voice will fill in the missing harmonic tones, reinforcing the harmonic implications of the original two voices.

3) The third voice may also complete open spots in the rhythmic pattern where desired.

EXAMPLE 126

*The two-voice counterpoint is found in the upper and lower voices, with the middle voice supplying contrast and harmonic and rhythmic definition.

4) In practice, the two voices written in two-voice counterpoint are not always the same ones. A frequent shifting of relationships is desired so that all voices remain equally important and significant.

Exercises in Three-Voice Writing

1) Add a third voice to the following two-voice examples.
2) Make this voice as interesting as possible.
3) Let it complete the harmonic implication of the other two voices.

a) Essential tones for this voice may be sketched in before the line is worked out fully.

b) Avoid the six-four chord unless it can be justified by rules of traditional harmony and *sounds well.*

4) It may complete the total rhythm where practical.
5) Let it take on the style of the two given voices as much as possible.

6) In some exercises, the given voices may change. It should be obvious where the added voice needs to be placed.

7) Weaker cadence patterns will be allowed in these exercises if they are considered to be fragments of larger passages.

MODEL 4

The given voices are in darker notes. The added voice is lighter to show how this exercise might be completed.

EXERCISE 15

4.

F maj.

5.

D maj.

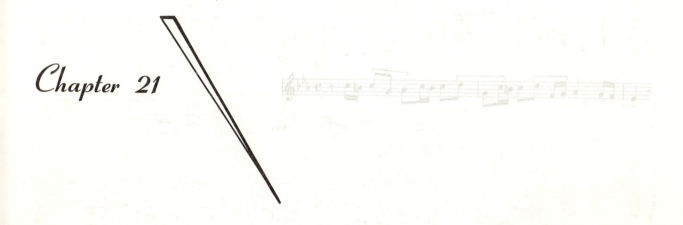

Chapter 21

Three-Voice Writing – B

In certain circumstances, it will be necessary to produce a three-voice texture by adding two voices to a single melodic line. Here, there could be two possible goals:

1) If the given line is rather slow moving, such as a chorale-style melody, then the added lines might be quite similar in movement and rather independent of the third except, of course, in harmonic relationships. In other words, this texture would give the effect of two-voice counterpoint written to elaborate, or accompany, a third line.

EXAMPLE 127

W. T. C. I, Fugue VIII

(The middle voice is the "leading" voice)

It would also be possible for one of the two added lines to coincide with the given line in two-voice counterpoint while the third voice could be more free.

EXAMPLE 128

(The upper voice is the "leading" voice)

2) In the case of a more active given line, it might be necessary for the two added voices to maintain the style and movement of the given voice, resulting in a more active overall setting. The best approach would be one of adding one line at a time for a beat or two, and then reinforcing this short two-voice setting with the third voice, changing relationships frequently.

EXAMPLE 129

(The lower voice is the "leading" voice)

Exercises with a Chorale Melody

1) The chorale line may be transposed to be used in any voice.
2) Imitative style between the two added voices is useful, or they may be rather parallel in structure.
3) Do not continue any parallel relationship (melodic or rhythmic) for more than two or three beats.
4) Decide on a tentative harmonization or harmonic background before beginning. Especially, decide on cadence points.
5) Try to write in a particular style.
6) These are only parts of chorales, so they may have endings with semicadences or modulations.

EXERCISE 16

1. "Mein Jesu, dem die Seraphinen"

2. "O du Liebe meiner Leibe"

3. "Gieb dich zufrieden"

4. "Jesu Leiden, Pein und Tod"

(8$^{\underline{va}}$ lower as middle voice)

5. "Wir glauben all' an einem Gott"

6. "Jesu, meine Freude"

7. "Herr Gott dich loben alle wir"

8. "Wachet auf, ruft uns die Stimme"

(8$^{\underline{va}}$ lower as middle voice) V

Exercises with an Active Voice

1) The purpose here is to produce similar style in all three voices.
2) The total rhythm must be kept in mind.
3) Imitative ideas to make all voices equally thematic should be used.
4) The given lines may be transposed to be used in any voice.
5) Beginning the added lines after rests occasionally may add interest and give independence.
6) When the given lines begin with a rest, one of the added voices must begin on the beat.

EXERCISE 17

Chapter 22

Three-Voice Writing – C

A third approach to writing in this texture will be that of elaborating three-voice harmony. Here, a harmonic sketch is used as the starting point and is elaborated and ornamented to conceal the vertical chords in the melodic lines.

The practical application of this approach will be found in working into cadences or accomplishing modulations where harmonic progression is of vital concern, thematic relationship becoming of secondary importance for the moment.

Exercises in Embellishing Three-Part Harmonic Sketches

It is not feasible to try to lead all three voices at once. The best procedure is to treat one voice at a time as a "leader" for no more than one to three beats, filling in the other two voices in procedures already described, and then transferring the lead to another voice. Generally this transfer will work out normally as a continuation of a melodic idea in one of the added voices.

It is possible, in embellishing the sparse three-part harmony, that missing chord tones may be inserted, chords made more complicated, or even harmonic implication changed where the overall progression is not noticeably disturbed. Rests at the entrance of some voices, and ties, are indispensable.

MODEL 5

Sketch

Elaboration

(Brackets indicate "leading" ideas)

EXERCISE 18

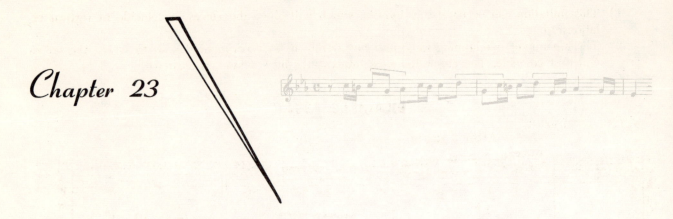

Chapter 23

Extended Contrapuntal Manipulation

In addition to the simple contrapuntal devices normally found in the Inventions and covered in Chapter 12, the more sophisticated contrapuntal forms such as the Fugue utilize other, more extended, ways of manipulating material in episode sections.

THE CANON IN THREE-VOICE TEXTURE

It is of course possible to have a three-voice canon as an extension of the techniques described in Chapter 11 on the two voice canon. A three-voice canon will have a "leader" and *two* "followers."

1) The first "follower" will duplicate in imitation what the "leader" has done, but a few beats later. The interval of imitation will be at the octave or the fifth, normally, and sometimes at the fourth. Other intervals are possible but become greatly more difficult.

2) The second "follower" will duplicate the first "follower" after the same rhythmic interval and at the same melodic interval as the first "follower" duplicates the "leader." This means that if the first "follower" is after three beats and at the interval of a fifth from the "leader," then the second "follower" will be after three beats and at the fifth from the first "follower," making its interval relationship with the leader a ninth (or a second). This is the way it would be measured.

3) Variances in the quality of intervals have to be made if voices appear on different scale steps in order to maintain the tonality.

The three-voice canon is not useful to us in any great degree as it is too difficult to handle as a device of development.

Canon in *two voices* is, however, very useful as a means of development within three-voice texture with the third voice either freely conceived or as a form of accompanying voice. This device is more commonly found in contrapuntal music of large dimensions.

As an example, Fugue VIII, beginning in measure 19, should be examined. The canon is in the two upper voices, the middle voice the "leader" beginning on the third beat. The upper voice follows after two beats at the octave. The voices have a free ending on the first beat of measure 24. The lower voice is free, completing the three-voice texture.

THE STRETTO

After a theme has been established for the listener, an effective device is that of its overlapping itself in imitation. In effect, the last part of the melodic idea becomes the counterpoint to the first part.

1) This imitation can occur at any interval which will allow the voices to coincide in vertical relationship.
2) The amount of overlapping must also be arrived at by experimentation as to where the voices will best coincide. The closer the time interval, the more tension is created.

EXAMPLE 130A

EXAMPLE 130B

3) A full three-voice stretto is very possible, but only with a carefully planned theme. This is not a matter of chance, but of forethought and hard work.
4) A stretto is considered complete when the first voice has completed its statement. More often than not, a three-voice stretto may not be completed at all, the important point being that *enough of each voice is heard with the characteristic part of the theme so that it is recognized by the listener.*

EXAMPLE 131

5) It is possible that one or more voices of a stretto may be inverted. This possibility (and place-ment) will again depend upon careful experimentation.

EXAMPLE 132

W. T. C. I, Fugue VI

As has been seen, often a two-voice stretto will appear in three-voice texture, either by itself as a con-trast in texture, or with a third voice added (usually free).

A stretto is actually completed when the first voice has finished its statement of the theme. Therefore, a stretto is never longer than a statement of the theme, and, as has been seen, may often be shorter. In contrast, a canon continues its imitation *beyond* the length of the original theme for a significant period of time.

AUGMENTATION

A statement of the theme in which the duration of the notes is *increased* is said to be an augmentation. The increase will be in *uniform ratio,* usually the value being doubled. This device works best in duple meters (although note values can be tripled). The result is a broadening, *grandioso* effect, perhaps most useful toward the end of a piece of music.

A note of warning: While a single voice may be broadened in this way, the other two voices of a three-voice texture must maintain the rhythmic pulse. A common practice is to allow each of the other voices one at a time to have a statement of the theme in its original rhythmic form, or a close derivation of it, at the same time that the augmentation occurs in the remaining voice.

1) This, of course, depends again on trial and error. Minor changes in the themes may be used to make them fit.
2) The point of entry of the other voices is free, depending upon the problem of obtaining the most agreement between the voices with the least amount of change.

Augmentation is also applied to all rests associated with the theme.

EXAMPLE 133

W. T. C. I, Fugue VIII

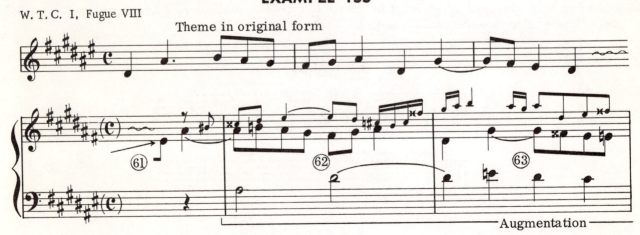

Lower voice: theme in augmentation
Middle voice: theme in original rhythm, measures 61-63
Upper voice: theme inverted, measures 64-66

DIMINUTION

A statement of a theme with note values consistently *shortened* (usually by half) is called a diminution. This device, with its effect of speeding up, is useful only in very particular cases, and usually only in duple meter. As with augmentation, the remaining voices must maintain the established rhythmic pulse or an uncomfortable speeding up will result. It is characteristically found only in pieces with slow themes. Seldom, if ever, will both augmentation and diminution be found in the same piece. This device can be said to be quite rare.

EXAMPLE 134

W. T. C. I, Fugue IX

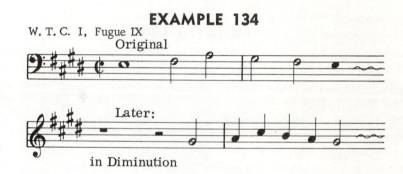

RETROGRESSION

This type of manipulation is also called "mirror" or "cancrizans," the latter being a word of Latin derivation meaning "crabwise." This device is included here not so much because of its degree of usefulness as to complete the student's vocabulary of contrapuntal devices. Retrogression is seldom found in the music of Bach. Examples appear in certain classical and romantic pieces, and it is an integral part of contemporary serial techniques, but it is rare in Bach.

In a mirror, or retrograde, manipulation, the theme in its original form is reversed, going from end to beginning, using the same intervals but in reverse order. As an illustration, a familiar example from Mozart's "Jupiter" Symphony will have to suffice.

EXAMPLE 135

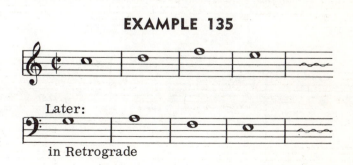

The reason for the lack of utilization of this device undoubtedly lies in the fact that it is almost impossible to recognize, sounding like a new theme, which can be disturbing to the continuity of the form in this style.

SHIFTED RHYTHM

Shifted rhythm is a device which can be used to subtly change emphasis on the notes of the theme, sometimes with fresh, interesting results, simply by placing the theme so that it will fall on different beats from the original. By shifting the theme forward or back one beat, a new arrangement of strong and weak values is placed on the notes of the melodic line. In a triple meter, even more possible variants of stress may be arrived at because of the one strong and two weak pulses in each measure.

EXAMPLE 136

W. T. C. I, Fugue XX
Original

Later:

Natural double counterpoint, covered in Chapter 13, is extremely useful within a three-voice texture, but will apply only to two voices still, with the third voice free.

Study Questions

1) Describe the most common use of the canon as a device of contrapuntal manipulation in three-voice texture.
2) What is the artistic principle of the stretto?
3) How is a stretto used?
4) What variants of the stretto are possible?
5) What is the difference between a stretto and a canon?
6) What is augmentation and what is its use?
7) What is diminution?
8) What are the other two names for retrograde manipulation?
9) Why is retrogression rare?
10) How is shifted rhythm used, and what is its value?

Exercises for Extended Manipulation

1) The following lines are to be rewritten in all possible manipulations as described in this Chapter.
2) Some lines will be found to be more adaptable to certain devices than others.
3) If the lines do not suit the device, experiments with minor alterations may be made.
4) The lines indicated by asterisk will be found to be adaptable to partial or full three-voice stretto.

EXERCISE 19

1. *

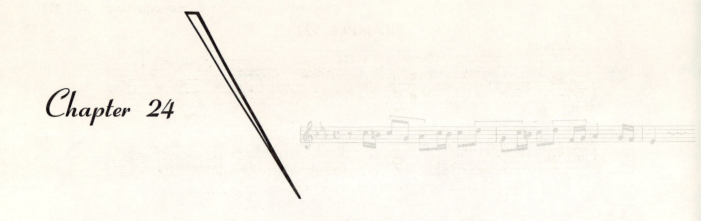

Chapter 24

The Sinfonias

The Sinfonias, or three-voice Inventions, seem to lie as a natural stylistic bridge between the simplicity of the two-voice Inventions and the sophistication of the Fugues.

THE MOTIVE

The **motives** of the Sinfonias are generally longer than those of the simplest two-voice Inventions — more akin to the motive of the lyric invention. (See Chapter 17, page 81.)

1) The motive is at least a measure in length, and sometimes two, or two-and-a-half measures long. It is a relatively complete musical thought with a weak feeling of cadence.

2) The motive begins within the tonic chord, either on the beat or after a short rest. The first note is most often the root of the tonic chord, or less frequently, the 5th. It is possible, but rare, to begin the motive on the 3rd of the tonic chord.

3) The motive ends on a strong beat, generally the first beat of the measure, although frequently, in a four-beat measure, it may be found to end on the third beat. (Compare motives of Sinfonias 1 and 2, with 3.)

4) The motive ends most frequently on the 3rd of the tonic chord, and this should be considered most desirable. Much less frequently, the root of the tonic chord, or the leading tone within dominant harmony may be used. (See motives of Sinfonias 7, 13, and 14.) Rarely, a motive may end on the 5th scale step, either as root of the dominant chord, or possibly the 5th of the tonic. (See motive of Sinfonia 3.)

5) Principles of melody writing and harmonic progression govern the content of the motive with the usual attempt to obtain a balance of rhythmic and melodic elements. The motive should contain distinguishing features which will make it easily recognizable, and will make possible interesting contrapuntal manipulations in the ensuing episodes.

THE EXPOSITION

The **exposition** of a Sinfonia is generally rather clear-cut in its design. Since the texture is three-voice, logical artistic principles call for an entrance of the motive to appear in each voice within the exposition.

EXAMPLE 137

1) The initial statement of the motive should be in either the upper or the middle voice. The lower voice should appear along with the initial statement as an accompanying bass-type line, strengthening the harmonic implications, and rhythmic characteristics of the motive.

   The initial statement and accompanying bass voice should end with the tonic chord, but can, though less frequently, end with the dominant. In either chord, the root should appear in the bass voice.

2) The second statement (first imitation) of the motive should appear in the other of the two higher voices, while the voice which had the initial statement will continue with a countermotive against the imitation. The countermotive follows the same principles as the countermotive of the two-voice Inventions, complementing the imitation of the motive melodically and rhythmically. This line may be thematically unimportant (a simple counterpoint), or may supply added material for later episodic manipulation. In most cases, the bass voice continues under the second statement of the motive, or it may drop out when the second voice enters. (See Sinfonia 2, third measure.)

   a) Occasionally, a few notes appear between the end of the first statement, and the beginning of the first imitation. If these notes appear to be in keeping with the material of the countermotive, they will be considered a part of it. In this case, then, the countermotive begins *before* the entrance of the second voice with its imitation.

EXAMPLE 138

(See also Sinfonia 13.)

   b) If these notes seem to be less significant than the countermotive which follows, then they should be considered to form a "melodic link" between the motive and the countermotive. This may consist of only one or two notes.

EXAMPLE 139

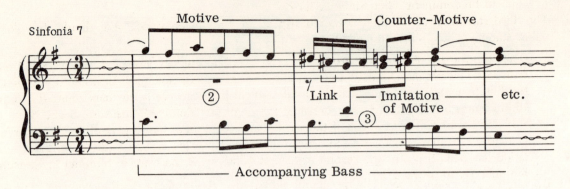

At the other extreme, the entire third measure of Sinfonia 15 would be a melodic link since it has nothing in common with the countermotive which follows.

c) The first imitation appears at the fifth from the original statement (a fifth higher, or a fourth lower). Although this imitation is "*at* the fifth," very rarely can it be said to be "*in* the dominant." Usually, every attempt is made to maintain tonic harmony at the beginning of this imitation in spite of the change of scale steps. This is necessary to avoid a feeling of modulation to the dominant at this point.

Certain inconsistencies found to occur between the motive and its imitation, involving the change of the size of one or more melodic intervals in the imitation, are necessary in order to *maintain the tonic harmony* through use of free imitation.

(1) Free imitation is accomplished by imitating one or more notes (usually involving the 5th scale step) at the *fourth* (fourth higher, or fifth lower) instead of at the normal fifth. It will be found *necessary* to apply this device when the motive begins on the 5th of the tonic chord.

(2) Such use of free imitation is warranted any time when the natural imitation implies dominant or subdominant harmonies too strongly, or when the end of the motive and the beginning of the imitation do not coincide harmonically.

EXAMPLE 140A

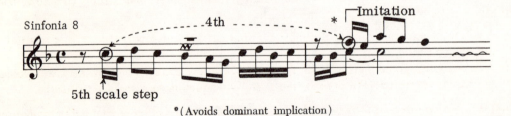

*(Avoids dominant implication)

EXAMPLE 140B

*(Avoids dominant implication, °vii)

(See also Sinfonia 1)

It is not necessary to make such changes if the harmony of the imitation is intended to be dominant. (See Sinfonia 7.)

3) The third statement of the motive should appear in the lower voice, and should be like the initial statement, an octave removed.

    a) Since the third statement appears in the tonic, and the second statement has probably ended within the dominant chord, it is usual for a bridge passage to appear between the second and third statements. The bridge usually is of two-voice texture with the bass omitted (Sinfonia 10, measures 5 and 6), but may consist of three voices (Sinfonia 7, measures 5 and 6).

    If it is found that the ending of the second statement and the beginning of the third can coincide, a bridge is not used (Sinfonia 1, measure 3). This is usually the case if a free imitation has been used for the second statement (Sinfonia 3, measure 6; Sinfonia 8, measure 3; Sinfonia 12, measure 5).

    b) The voice which has just completed the second statement of the motive continues against the third statement with the material of the countermotive, or some similar line.

    c) The voice which first announced the motive presents further new material. This is called the *second counterpoint,* and may be relatively unimportant as regards later development.

    d) The end of the third announcement of the motive concludes the normal exposition, and, as in the two-voice Inventions, the last chord is used to make an elision into the first episode.

THE EPISODES

The **episodes** are formed as sections of development of the ideas presented in the exposition, using the same techniques and devices as were used in the two-voice Inventions.

1) All three voices must participate in the development of ideas.
2) Natural double counterpoint between two of the three voices is very common (Sinfonia 12, compare upper voices in measure 5 with upper voices in measure 24).
3) Occasionally, a new counterpoint will appear in the episode of the second section. (See Sinfonia 7, measure 14, and on. The sixteenth-note movement is constant from this point to the end of the Sinfonia.)

THE FORM

In **form,** the Sinfonias tend to be much more free than the two-voice Inventions. Sectional form is adhered to, but the number of sections varies greatly, and the sections are not always defined by a strong, obvious cadence. Sections may be found to be defined by factors other than strong cadences, such as the appearance of:

    a) A different manipulation of the motive (Sinfonia 14, measure 12 — a brief, partial stretto in the two upper voices).
    b) A new counterpoint (Sinfonia 13, measure 21 — new counterpoint in the lower voice).
    c) A change of texture(Sinfonia 8, measure 7 — reduction to two-voice texture).

1) The use of a counter-exposition at the beginning of a new section is relatively common, and is not necessarily restricted to use at the beginning of the second section, as was found in the two-voice Inventions. Two statements are usually enough, although three may be found where this does not lead to a monotonous repeating of the motive. (See Sinfonia 7, measure 14 through measure 17. The lower voice does not participate. In measures 25 through 28, another counterexposition appears, using upper and lower voices.) The texture is not reduced beyond two voices.
2) The number of sections in the Sinfonias varies greatly.

    a) *Three-section* structure, as was found in the two-voice Inventions, is frequent. (See Sinfonia 9 with *major* dominant used for third section, and also Sinfonia 6.)
    b) Quite often, a *four-section* structure seems to be preferred, with the fourth section returning to the tonic. (See Sinfonia 12 with cadence to dominant in measure 9, cadence to relative minor in measure 15, cadence to tonic in measure 24.)

(1) The fourth section can be an added section to the already established three-section form, as in Sinfonia 12.

(2) The fourth section may also result from the subdivision of a longer section by a strong cadence. (See Sinfonia 8, second section at the third beat of measure 7. A strong cadence to the supertonic [ii] at the third beat of measure 11 subdivides the second section of a three-section form. The normal third section [now the fourth] is indicated by a cadence to the relative minor at the third beat of measure 15.)

(3) Four sections may also be arrived at in the same manner, by subdividing both parts of a basic two-section form.

   c) The technique of forming the sections of the Sinfonia around a single statement of the motive followed by a short episode leads to any number of short sections, each with its own cadence. (See Chapter 17, page 80.)

  3) *Cadences* used to define sections in the Sinfonias are not always the expected ones. Greater freedom in the choice of cadence is allowed. The supertonic (ii) chord may be used as the goal of a cadence, and also the chord on the lowered leading tone (VII) is found frequently. The subdominant (iv or IV) is quite common.

It would seem that the strength of the cadence and changes in the handling of material are more important in defining sections than any set pattern of cadences. The main concern is that the cadences give balanced contrasts and are arrived at logically.

Variants from the most frequent patterns, as discussed above, exist.

  1) The third statement of the motive in the exposition is sometimes at the fifth, like the second statement. (See Sinfonia 6, first three measures.)

  2) The exposition may consist of only two entrances of the motive, both tonic, going immediately into episode, omitting the third entrance. A logical resolution of this exception is for the displaced third entrance to appear prominently at the beginning of the second section in the dominant (as in Sinfonia 2, third beat of measure 9) or in the relative key (as in Sinfonia 15, measure 14).

  3) Sinfonia 5 is avoided completely in this study because it is really a two-voice invention with an accompanying bass line, in the manner of a trio sonata, and is not of the same genre as the other Sinfonias.

The earliest known manuscript of the Sinfonias, as they appeared in the *"Little Clavier Book for Wilhelm Friedemann Bach,"*[1] reveals that the composer at first chose to call each by the name of "Fantasia," indicating a much greater freedom in his approach to their composition. The apparently loose structure of the Sinfonias as compared with the greater adherence to pattern in the two-voice Inventions can be understood only from the musical viewpoint and justified only by valid principles of musical expression.

Study Questions

1) What are the characteristics of the motive of a Sinfonia?
2) On what note will the motive best begin?
3) At what rhythmic point, and on what note, will the motive best end?
4) How many entrances of the motive are normally found within the exposition?
5) In which voices may the initial entrance of the motive appear?
6) Describe the function of the lowest voice at the beginning of the Sinfonia.
7) Where, and at what interval, will the first imitation of the motive appear?
8) What inconsistencies may be allowed in the first imitation? Why are these necessary?
9) What happens in the other two voices against the first imitation?
10) In which voice will the third entrance of the motive appear? At what interval of imitation?
11) What happens in the other two voices against the third entrance?

---

[1]Ralph Kirkpatrick, Preface to facsimile edition of the "Clavier-Büchlein vor Wilhelm Friedemann Bach" by J. S. Bach, Yale University Press, 1959.

12) Discuss the desirability of using a bridge between the second and third entrances. When is this necessary?

13) What devices commonly appear in the episodes of the Sinfonias?

14) What general statement can be made concerning the form of the Sinfonias?

15) Explain the differences in form, and how they are arrived at.

Analysis

1) Analyze, in chart form, several of the Sinfonias in the manner of Chapter 15.

2) The second counterpoint may be represented by the following symbol:

∨ ∨ ∨ ∨ ∨ ∨ — second counterpoint

∧ ∧ ∧ ∧ ∧ ∧ — material derived from second counterpoint

3) Pay particular attention to the overall form, and the sectional structure.

4) Suggested for special attention are Sinfonias 2, 6, 7, 9, 12, and 13, although all (except 5) are worthy of study.

Exercises for Writing

1) Write expositions for three-voice Sinfonias using several of the following motives. Use links and bridges if, and where, necessary.

EXERCISE 20

2) Extend one or more of the expositions worked out for 1), above, into a complete Sinfonia after the style of the Sinfonias of Bach, or,

3) Write original motives and use as the basis for writing a Sinfonia as above.

Let The Well-Tempered Clavier *be your daily meat. Then
you will certainly become a
solid musician.*
—Robert Schumann

Part IV

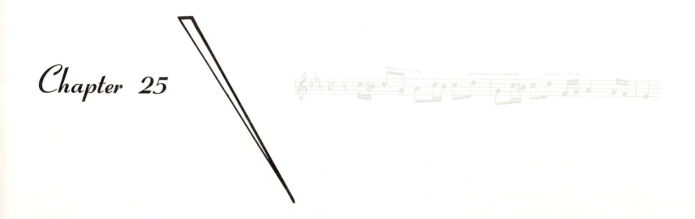

Chapter 25

The Three-Voice Fugue – A

The fugue is the most sophisticated of the various forms of counterpoint. Although its basic principles are found in the great Flemish school of contrapuntal writing as early as the fifteenth century and are an integral part of the motets of Josquin des Près, the fugue did not mature until the seventeenth century with the line of composers leading to and culminating in J. S. Bach.

Bach can be given almost total credit for the standardization of structure and practices of the fugue as we know it. His more highly developed contrapuntal skills and more inherent feeling for balance and form, along with his incomparable artistic gifts, place his fugal efforts far above any others of his time or since, and make his fugues models for composers to this day.

The fugue is a larger work than the invention and can be said to be more "serious" in content. In practice, it is still a piece of music based on the imitation and development of a melodic idea along the lines seen in the inventions, but in a more extended way. There are certain specific limitations and stylistic requirements which set the fugue apart from other imitative contrapuntal forms, but in a general way, it can be said that the structure of the fugue in its simpler form follows the principles seen in the inventions.

1) The fugue begins with an exposition in which the main thematic material is stated and imitated in all the voices with appropriate counterpoints in the other voices to complete the texture.
2) The rest of the fugue is extremely free as far as what may happen is concerned. Basically, it can be said that it consists of episodes and restatements of the theme with a harmonic plan similar to that which was found in the inventions.

THE SUBJECT

The theme of a fugue is called a "subject." This is a more extended musical idea than the motive of an invention. It has a rather definite cadence, which rounds it off as a full musical phrase, or even sometimes a period, ending, of course, on a strong beat. (Compare with Chapter 14, page 65.)

1) If it is to be a period, a weaker cadence will appear at the approximate middle, dividing it into two phrases.
2) The subject may be only a few beats long, but will contain harmonic progression.

EXAMPLE 141

3) Or, it may be as long as several measures.

EXAMPLE 142

(Some of Bach's organ fugues have even longer subjects of six to eight, or more, measures.)

The subject begins with a definition of tonic harmony, either at or very near the beginning. It may begin on the root (strongest), or 3rd of the tonic chord, or it may begin on the 5th scale step, either as root of the dominant chord or as 5th of the tonic.

1) Movement *from* the 5th scale step appearing at or near the beginning of the subject must be *upward by step or skip,* or *downward by skip only,* for reasons which will be apparent in the next Chapter.
2) Very rarely the subject can begin on the 3rd of the dominant chord (the leading tone), generally as a "pick-up" beat.
3) The tonic note appears near, if not at, the beginning. There are numerous exceptions to this, but this practice is the safest.

The subject may begin on a strong beat, or a weak beat, or after a short rest.

1) In a subject beginning on a weak beat, this beat will usually function as a "pick-up" beat to the next strong beat. If the tonic note does not occur on this beat, the tonic should appear on the first succeeding strong beat.
2) It is quite frequent that the subject begin after a short rest to make the line begin on the weak part of a strong beat.

Since the subject has the structure of a phrase (or period), harmonic progression is necessary.

1) The implied harmonic content will be simple and strong. Subordinate harmonies should be kept to a minimum, except possibly as nonfunctional chords (the result of voice leading).
2) Definition of the phrase is accomplished by the use of a cadence formula at the end. It need not be a strong cadence, but strong enough to give a feeling of temporary rest or conclusion to the line.
3) Modulation is possible within a subject, but normally it will return to the original key at its end.

The subject will end on the root or 3rd of the tonic chord (more commonly the 3rd), or the dominant note as the 5th of the tonic harmony.

1) It is possible for a subject to modulate to the dominant key at its close, in which case, it would end on the new tonic, or the mediant of the new key.
2) Other cadences are possible, but very rare.
3) Rhythmically, the final note of the subject will appear on a strong beat as a logical cadence ending of a phrase.

The subject may be announced first in any voice, but will be alone.

Analysis of Subjects

1) Since this Part will deal with only the three-voice fugues, analysis will be restricted to these. However, it would be desirable to examine all of the fugue subjects at hand, and this is strongly recommended.

2) The three-voice Fugues in Volume I of the *Well-Tempered Clavier* are: II, III, VI, VII, VIII, IX, XI, XIII, XV, XIX, XXI.

3) Make a chart consisting of eight columns and analyze, by completing this chart, the subjects of the three-voice Fugues in Book I of the *Well-Tempered Clavier,* as in the following illustration.

Number of Fugue and key	Scale step on which Subject begins	Chord with which Subject begins	Beat or fraction on which it begins	Length of Subject	Beat on which Subject ends	Scale step on which Subject ends	Chord with which Subject ends
II - c minor	1st	tonic	last half of 1	2 meas. and 1 beat	1st	3rd	tonic

Study Questions

1) What are the basic characteristics of a fugue?
2) What is a "subject"?
3) What general characteristics exist in a subject?
4) How does a subject differ from a motive?
5) In what ways may a subject begin?
6) How should a subject end?
7) Discuss modulation in terms of a subject.
8) From your analysis, what is the most frequent beginning note and chord for a subject?
9) From your analysis, what can be determined about the rhythmic characteristics of the beginning of a subject?
10) What is the average length of the subjects which you analyzed?
11) How many subjects are found to end on weak beats?
12) From your analysis, what can be determined about the scale step and chord to appear at the end of a subject?

Exercise for Writing

Write several subjects in varied styles and keys according to the principles determined from the foregoing analysis.

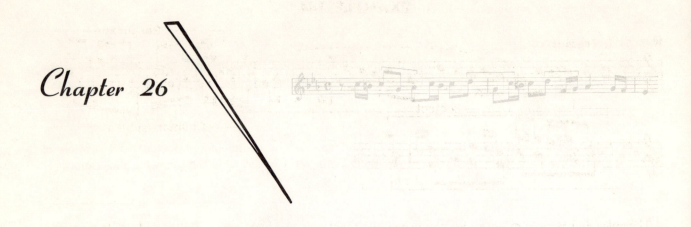

Chapter 26

The Three-Voice Fugue – B

The next occurrence in the exposition of a fugue is the imitation of the subject. In a fugue, the first imitation is called the **response** (or "answer"). As the second voice imitates the subject with its response, the first voice continues with a counterpoint against the response. The continuation in the first voice is called the **countersubject**.

THE RESPONSE

The most characteristic feature of the fugue is the treatment afforded the first imitation in the exposition, which is at the interval of the fifth from the initial statement (fifth above or fourth below). In the three-voice fugues, the response occurs in an *adjacent* voice to the one which has made the first statement of the subject. Stylistic practice (in addition to practical harmonic considerations) dictates certain very definite treatments for this entrance.

1) When all notes of the response are found to be a fifth above (or a fourth below) the corresponding notes of the subject, then the response is said to be *real*.

EXAMPLE 143

This is the normal practice unless certain conditions prevail to require a different handling.

2) If certain notes of the response are found to be fourth above (or a fifth below) the corresponding notes of the subject, then the response is said to be *tonal*. There may be only one such note, or sometimes more.

EXAMPLE 144

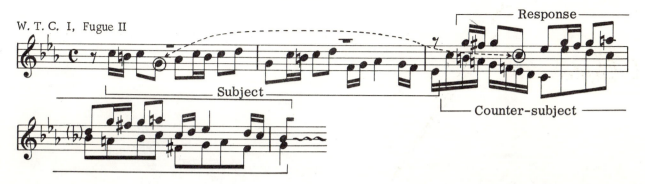

The rules and principles governing the use of the tonal response are very definite, and all involve the appearance of the *dominant note within the subject.*

1) If the subject *begins* on the dominant note (fifth scale step), then that note must be "imitated tonally" in the response.

   a) The dominant note at the beginning of the subject will be imitated in the response a fourth higher (fifth lower) instead of the normal fifth higher (or fourth lower).

   b) Only this single note will be so treated, the rest of the line being imitated at the fifth.

EXAMPLE 145

2) If the subject contains a prominent dominant note *near the beginning,* this note will be "imitated tonally" (a fourth above or a fifth below) in the response.

   a) Again, usually only the one note is affected.

   b) "Near" can be defined as including the second, third, or fourth notes of the subject.

EXAMPLE 146

3) If the subject *ends* on the dominant note and this note is heard as the *root of the dominant chord* instead of as the fifth of the tonic, then this note must be "imitated tonally."

   a) In this case, a fine distinction must be drawn. In the following example, the final note of the subject is heard as the 5th of the tonic chord because of the natural leaning of the implied harmony before it (°vii⁷ demanding tonic as a resolution). Therefore the response is *real*.

EXAMPLE 147

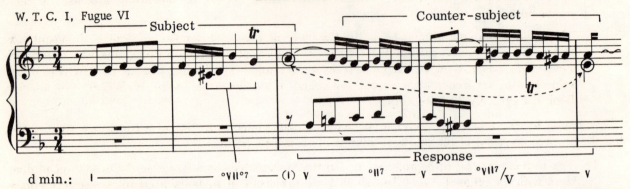

(The fact that the minor dominant is the harmony used in the third measure has nothing to do with the natural harmonic implications in the subject. The 5th scale step may belong to either tonic or dominant chords, its final implication being determined by context.)

   b) In the following example, the dominant note at the end of the subject is definitely heard as the root of the dominant chord, even as the goal of a modulation to the dominant key, because of the strong V⁷/V implication in the last half of the subject. In this case, the note *is* "imitated tonally."

EXAMPLE 148

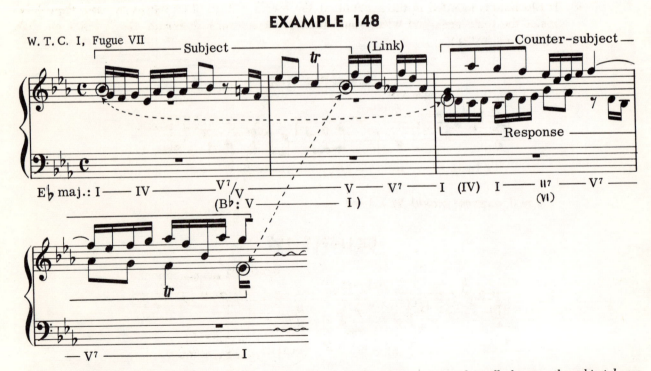

Here, certain further explanation is necessary. The first note of the subject is imitated tonally because the subject *began* on the dominant note (see 1, above). In addition to the last note, the entire last half of the subject is imitated tonally because the strong harmonic association of a secondary dominant (F A C E♭) to its tonic (B♭), (V⁷/V to V), at the end of the subject, is so potent that it must be duplicated in the response, so the tonal imitation of the last note (E♭) calls for a B♭ D F A♭ chord (V⁷ to I) to precede it. The eighth rest makes a convenient breaking point so that this change may occur smoothly.

4) In addition to the individual dominant notes appearing in the subject which must be answered tonally in the response, there are occasions when certain notes closely associated with these dominants may also need to be imitated in the same manner.

    a) Turns, mordents, and other ornamentations would become meaningless if dissociated from the note to which they are applied.

    b) As shown in Example 148, certain harmonic affinities sometimes require total imitation of more than just the single note.

    c) No characteristic rhythmic or melodic movement should be noticeably affected by these changes.

5) The leading tone, not often used as the first note of a subject, implies, of course, dominant harmony, but does not require a tonal response because of its strong melodic function. (See *Well-Tempered Clavier*, Book II, Fugue XIII, as an example.) The leading tone as the last note of the subject (also not frequent) is usually not imitated tonally either. (See *Well-Tempered Clavier*, Book I, Fugue XV, as an example.)

The reason for the tonal response as a characteristic part of the exposition of a fugue is a stylistic one, but the practice grew out of the practical solution of an artistic problem.

1) The response at the fifth produces an artistically desirable contrast, within the exposition, of dominant with the original tonic. The fact that the subject of a fugue is a complete musical phrase, with a significant harmonic structure strongly stressing the tonic key, leads to the artistic problem.

2) A melodic line which is strongly centered around the tonic will be equally as strongly centered around the dominant when reproduced at the fifth, as in a response. Contrast is desirable, but a sudden shift of tonal center so early in a piece is too abrupt. The response should imply the *dominant of the original key — not a new key.* Tonal response, then, resolves the question of weakening this implication when it is too strong.

3) The element which leads to this difficulty is the dominant note (5th of the tonic chord) at, or near, the beginning of the subject.

    a) If this note is imitated in the response at the fourth instead of at the usual fifth, then it becomes the tonic note, and what would have been a strong dominant chord takes on tonic implication instead.

EXAMPLE 149

A real response would have been

EXAMPLE 150

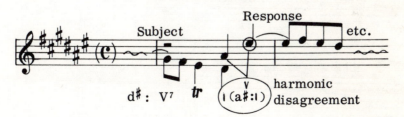

A tonal response gives

EXAMPLE 151

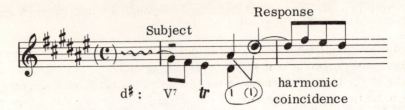

b) This smoothes the entry into the response harmonically but still allows, basically, the contrast of an imitation at the fifth.

4) The same danger exists with a dominant note at the end of the subject as root of dominant harmony. Reproduced at the fifth, as in a real response, this dominant note would become supertonic, implying the root of the ii chord — a rather undesirable implication in such an important position. Imitating the dominant note at the fourth instead of at the usual fifth brings the response to a close on tonic harmony — a much more palatable situation.

a) If an actual modulation to the dominant has taken place, then it will be necessary to maintain the harmonic association as shown in Example 148.

b) Sometimes the adjustment is not so easily made as in the above-quoted example. It can be made at any point at which satisfactory harmonic implications and melodic characteristics can be maintained.

(1) Often the size of an interval may be changed, but the harmonic implication must be checked when this is done.

(2) Sometimes, it is necessary to use a repeated note in place of stepwise movement, or vice verse, but this is best *after* the strong part of a beat.

(3) Several notes may need to be changed to maintain a coherent line.

EXAMPLE 152

W. T. C. I, Fugue XXIII

(4) No rules can be made for this adjustment other than that it must sound natural and must not materially change the shape of the melodic line nor introduce undesirable harmonic implications.

There are many exceptions to the use of the tonal response, each a special case with individual conditions.

1) If the dominant key is not too strong in the response, it can sometimes be covered with a well-planned countersubject, and a real response used.
2) Some exceptional rhythmic placements of the dominant element, as it appears in the response, may allow it to be treated as a dominant of the original key, progressing to the tonic on the next beat, and a real response used.
3) It is best for the learner not to become involved in experimentation. All exception must be based on artistic choice, which is developed through experience and practice.

Analysis of Responses

Make a chart in the manner of the one used for analysis of the subjects. Use seven columns and analyze the responses of the three-voice Fugues in Volume I, *Well-Tempered Clavier*. Compare this analysis with the chart of subjects for the same Fugues.

Number of Fugue and key	Scale step on which Response begins	Chord with which Response begins	Scale step on which Response ends	Chord with which Response ends	Type of Response	If tonal, where is change made?
II - c minor	5th	tonic	7th (lowered bt.)	minor dom.	tonal	near beginning (4th note)

Study Questions

1) What is the response in a fugue?
2) Why is the response so important in a fugue?
3) What conditions prevail in the subject when it may be imitated with a real response?
4) When is it necessary to use a tonal response?
5) How is this accomplished?
6) From your analysis, how frequent is this form of response?
7) Explain the conditions that lead to the different treatments of the dominant note at the end of the subject when imitated in the response.
8) How much of a response needs to be tonal?
9) Why is a tonal response necessary?
10) From your analysis, when a tonal response is required, where is the change most frequently necessary?

Exercises for Writing

1) Write responses for the subjects written for Chapter 25.
2) Write responses for the following subjects:

EXERCISE 21

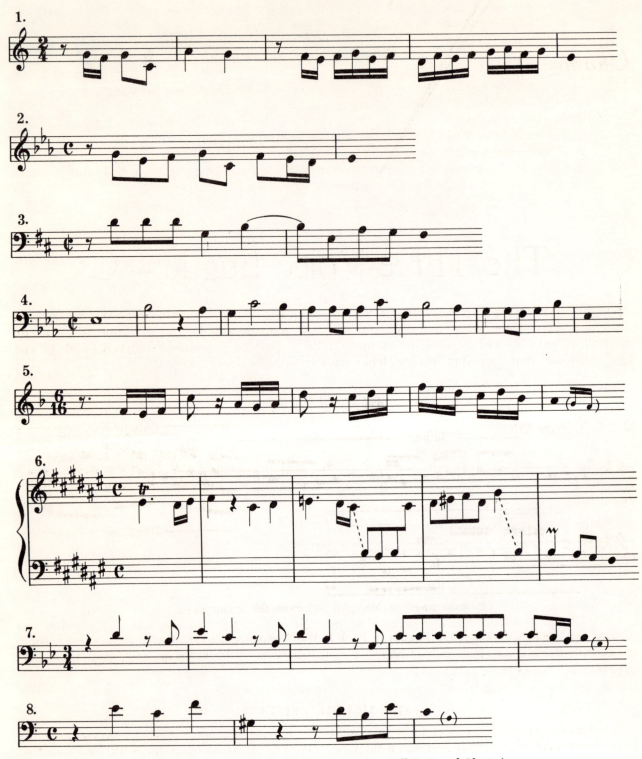

(These subjects are all from Book II of Bach's *Well-Tempered Clavier*.)

Chapter 27

The Three-Voice Fugue – C

The **countersubject** is the continuation of the first voice as a counterpoint to the response. This line is of value in reinforcing the harmonic implications of the response and in helping to define and maintain rhythmic patterns, as well as providing an opportunity to introduce some new, contrasting melodic and rhythmic ideas, thus supplying more material for later episodic development.

EXAMPLE 153

(At least three new ideas can be seen in this countersubject.)

All of the countersubjects of the Fugues in Book I, *Well-Tempered Clavier,* should be examined, noticing their rhythmic and melodic characteristics as compared to the subjects (responses) with which they appear.

THE MELODIC BRIDGE

The third entrance of the subject in the exposition (the second imitation), is at the octave from the original statement. This centers it again on the tonic. Since the response is at the fifth, and therefore centered around the dominant, it is probable that it will end with an implied dominant harmony (if the subject ended with tonic).

It would be impossible, in this situation, to attempt a tonic entrance immediately at the end of the response because it would lead to a conflict of tonic and dominant harmonies. It is the custom, at this point, to insert a two-voice *melodic bridge* to lead the implied harmony back to tonic at the correct rhythmic point for the entrance of the third voice.

1) The bridge is usually constructed of material derived from the subject (response) and the countersubject which have just preceded it.

EXAMPLE 154

Upper voice: derived from subject
Middle voice: derived by inversion from countersubject

2) Sometimes a new melodic idea may be introduced, but it must be a logical continuation of what has gone before.

3) The length of the bridge varies greatly. Usually it is not longer than the subject itself. With a short subject, however, it can be longer. It is most often of about the same duration as the subject, or a little shorter. The real determinant of length is that the third voice enter at the *same rhythmic point* as the initial statement of the subject, so the bridge must fill in to that point.

   There is no real hurry evidenced in Bach's Fugues. A temporary delay in the entrance of the third voice seems to be used, sometimes, to make this entrance more dramatic and forceful through the element of suspense.

4) If the subject ends with dominant harmony, requiring a tonal response, the response will end with tonic harmony, and the third voice may enter immediately without a bridge.

5) Sometimes, apparently for artistic effect, Bach inserts a bridge even if it is not needed. At other times, a bridge may seem to be needed, but if the subject begins on the dominant note, and is properly placed, the bridge may be eliminated as long as the harmonic progression is natural and not rushed in feeling. (See Chapter 26, page 127.)

EXAMPLE 155

6) It may occur that a bridge is not needed for harmonic reasons, but is used simply to get to the proper *rhythmic point* for the re-entry of the subject in the third voice. In Fugue VII (q. v.) the response ends on the tonic harmony in measure 4, but on the third beat. Bach chose to use a bridge a measure and a half in length so that the third voice enters on the strong beat of measure 6. In this Fugue, there is a rather exceptional melodic bridge of almost two beats between the subject and the response, necessitated by the fact that the response is tonal at both ends, the subject beginning on the dominant note and modulating to the dominant chord at the end.

7) The material found in the bridge may be used rather prominently in later episodic passages, or it may not be seen again.

THE THIRD ENTRANCE

To fulfill the principle of the unity of voices, the remaining voice now makes its statement of the subject. The third entrance (which is the second imitation) is like the initial statement of the subject, in a different octave (imitation at the octave). The completion of this statement ends the normal exposition of a three-voice fugue, giving the pattern of subject-response-subject to the exposition.

1) Along with this statement of the subject, the countersubject is moved to the second voice (which stated the response). This may be the same line, but of course on different scale steps, or it may be only a similar line, either derived, ornaménted, or, sometimes, simplified.

2) The first voice, which originally announced the subject, will now have a new line completing the three-voice texture. The new line is called the *second counterpoint*.

a) It completes and reinforces the two-voice counterpoint formed by the subject and the counter-subject.

b) Often it is less active than the other two. Its purpose is to supply melodic and rhythmic contrast, in addition to supporting the harmonic implications.

c) The second counterpoint is of varying importance. In some fugues, it may make its only appearance in the exposition while in others, it may supply some melodic or rhythmic idea that proves to be very useful in the episodic passages that follow.

EXAMPLE 156

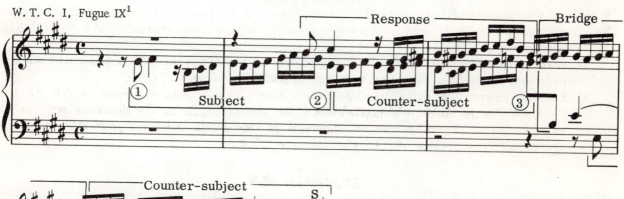

---

[1]An exceptional point in this Fugue is the slight overlapping of the first imitation and the initial statement of the subject (measure 2, second and third beats). Some writers eliminate this apparent discrepancy by saying that the subject ends on the *b* (third sixteenth note of the second beat). This is the weak part of a beat, and the 5th of the tonic chord — two unlikely occurrences in view of previous discoveries. The subject, as a melodic phrase, does not complete itself logically until the *e* on the third beat of measure 2. Therefore, it seems that this is the end of the subject, and that the overlapping is the result of the fact that the subject begins on the last half of the second beat as a "pick-up" rhythmically to the stronger third beat. The overlapping, then, is necessary to avoid a disturbing shift in rhythm which would occur if the first imitation were to appear a beat later. Corroboration for this occurrence can be found in the exposition of two-voice Invention 3 (which see).

The apparent discrepancy in rhythmic placement of the third statement (measure 4) as compared with the other two can be explained if it is noticed that this placement allows the third statement, *and* the exposition, to *end* on the *first* beat of a measure (measure 5).

THE EXPOSITION

The foregoing describes in detail the structure of the exposition of a three-voice fugue.

1) The exposition normally consists of three entrances of the "theme" in subject-response-subject (tonic-dominant-tonic) relationship. As has been seen, the exposition also presents the countersubject and the second counterpoint in their appropriate places.

2) The purpose of an exposition is to present the thematic material and to introduce and define each of the voices which will be responsible for the manipulation and development of the material for the duration of the fugue.

3) Occasionally a fourth entrance of the subject occurs in a three-voice fugue in such a clear manner that it must be included as an extension of the exposition. When this happens, the new entrance occurs as another response (at the fifth), an octave removed from the second statement.

   a) In common practice, two entrances do not follow each other in the same voice unless a melodic bridge separates them.

   b) Actually, there is no special place for a fourth statement. It may occur in any voice, but is usually found in either of the two strongest voices, the upper or lower.

   c) An example of the four-entrance exposition in a three-voice fugue may be found in Fugue VIII. The fourth entrance appears in the lowest voice, measures 12 — 14 (augmentation of the next-to-last note). It follows a five-beat melodic bridge in three voices to separate it from the third entrance, which also appeared in the lowest voice.

   d) The fourth entrance generally will be found only in fugues of more significant proportions.

Study Questions

1) What is the location and function of the countersubject?
2) When is a melodic bridge needed, and where?
3) How long should the melodic bridge be?
4) What is the interval of imitation for the third entrance?
5) What occurs in the other voices with the third entrance?
6) What is the purpose of an exposition?
7) What is the content of the exposition of a three-voice fugue?
8) When and how is it possible to have four entrances of the subject material in the exposition of a three-voice fugue?

Assignments

1) Add countersubjects to some of the responses written for Chapter 26. Carry them through the third entrance and a complete three-voice exposition.

2) Write original subjects in a variety of styles and tonalities and extend them into complete expositions.

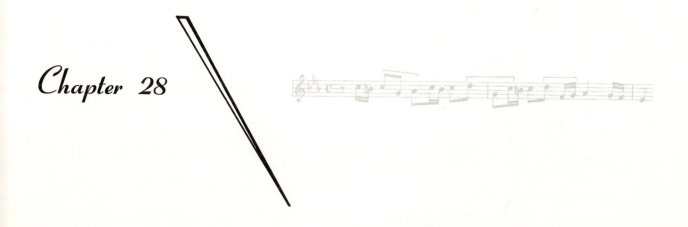

Chapter 28

The Three-Voice Fugue – D

In the manner of the Inventions and Sinfonias, the exposition of a fugue is followed by an **episode** in which the materials of the subject, the countersubject, sometimes the second counterpoint, and the melodic bridge, if it is independent material, are developed and manipulated.

1) The episode immediately following the exposition is usually simpler in content than those which follow, using the devices of simple contrapuntal manipulation for the most part. In a more complex fugue, it is possible that the device of stretto may be found this early.

2) The episode is modulatory, moving to and ending in a next-related key. In the Fugues, as in the Sinfonias, it is not as common that perfect authentic cadences be used at the ends of episodes. Fugue episodes tend to blend into ensuing sections more than those found in the Inventions.

   a) The most distinguishing characteristic defining the appearance of a new section is the reappearance of the subject as a statement, an obvious change in the type of development used, or a change of texture.

   b) Counterexpositions, as such, are rare in the simpler fugues, but a statement of the subject at the beginning of a section is frequent.

3) The later episodes following the first will become progressively more complicated, using more sophisticated devices of development as the fugue progresses.

THE FORM

It is wrong, actually, to use the term "form" in connection with a fugue. A fugue *has* form in that the presentation of material is balanced and progressive, and there is a definite key plan, but it is not *a form* in itself. A fugue may appear in virtually any musical structure from the simplest of the part forms to song forms, rondos, or even the largest sonata (sonata-allegro) and fantasia forms.

The structure of an individual fugue is based upon a key plan and the restatement of the subject, with subsequent developments of the material of the exposition. The most common design found in fugues of moderate length is the sectional form, basically the same as was seen in the Inventions. This form gives the composer the element of defined points of harmonic contrast, and sectionalizing tends to give order to his developments.

1) Basically, the key plan is the same as that found in the Inventions for the two-section and three-section forms.

2) Fugues sometimes appear to have a greater number of sections, but the larger sectional forms are usually found, on closer examination, to be subdivisions of the familiar two- and three-section forms. Two apparently separate sections often will be subdivisions of one larger section, held together by common use of material.

Since cadences may be weaker (although they *will* be present), the most dependable signs to look for, in differentiating sections, are restatements of the subject and differing means of developing the material, coinciding with an implied change of tonal center.

After the exposition is passed, there is extreme freedom in the planning of the fugue (although planning must be done). It is common that certain episodic passages may assume importance second only to the subject, and may reappear several times in the course of the fugue.

Analysis

1) Analyze in diagram form, thematically and harmonically, the three-voice Fugues in Book I, *Well-Tempered Clavier*.
2) Use the symbols given in Chapter 15, page 73 (for analysis of the Invention) in addition to the symbols for the second counterpoint as given in Chapter 24, page 114.
3) Follow the same procedure as with the Inventions.
4) Indicate and number the sections as you find them.

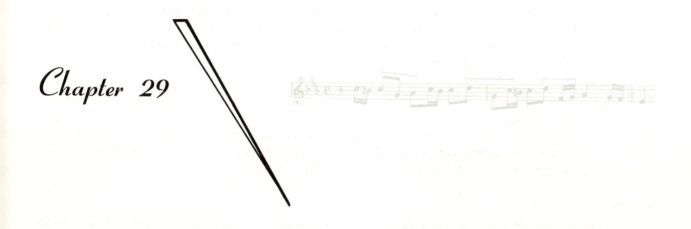

Chapter 29

Writing a Three-Voice Fugue

In writing a fugue, the best teacher is the master, himself. Constant referral to the three-voice Fugues of Bach will solve most of the problems that arise. It is recommended that the student model his work, even to use of the general harmonic scheme and order of the use of developmental devices, after the Bach Fugues. It must be pointed out, however, that what can be done with one subject may not be possible with another, so the "modeling" must be in general principle only.

For the purposes of this study of the eighteenth-century fugue, it is desirable to arrive at a subject which can be manipulated in as many ways as possible, particularly in three-voice stretto. In this respect, not just any subject will work in three-voice stretto. True, not all, nor even most, of Bach's Fugues contain a three-voice stretto, but for the practice it will give in contrapuntal manipulation, a student's should, if possible.

It is probable that when Bach conceived the subject for a fugue, he foresaw immediately its possibilities and limitations from the standpoint of contrapuntal manipulation. Bach's judgment grew out of his phenomenal improvisational abilities, his highly developed skill, and experience. These gifts and skills are lost to all but a few, so trial and error, or cold-blooded calculation and planning must be substituted, perhaps at the expense of elements of spontaneity.

In order to write a fugue with a subject which will work in three-voice stretto, a subject must be produced by *writing* a three-voice stretto. The chances of writing a melodic line that will happen to work in three-voice stretto are very slim, indeed. To attempt this procedure is to court madness. For this reason, the first step should be to write a three-voice stretto (really a short three-voice canon at a very close time interval), and remove the "leader" to use as the subject of the fugue.

1) This will present certain difficulties, the first being to conduct the "leader" in such a way as to produce a respectable melodic line with all the characteristics of a good fugue subject.
2) The next difficulty is that of obtaining an acceptable harmonic progression, requiring careful maneuvering at as close a time interval as this "canon" must be.
3) There is one redeeming point: the imitations in the stretto, while they must be the same distance apart rhythmically, may be at any melodic interval and may even be slightly altered, as a last resort.

   a) The interval of the octave for these imitations is the safest except for the matter of range of voices (encouraging undesirable crossed voices), and the danger of static harmony.
   b) A combination of fourth or fifth for the first imitation and octave for the second sometimes works well.

     c) Intervals of a second and third are not impossible in these imitations, but may give harmonic difficulties.

  4) The stretto (or canon) must be strict for a sufficient enough time to allow each voice to become recognizable as an imitation of the original line. In this respect, if a full length stretto does not seem possible after a reasonable number of tries, it may be necessary to be content with a partial stretto (see Example 131), completing the subject line independently.

After a subject has been produced in the manner described above, the "leader" should be removed from the stretto and tested melodically and harmonically to determine whether or not it will stand up as a workable fugue subject and as a good musical expression. The subject should be tried in enough of the different means of contrapuntal manipulations (simple and extended) to determine that it will be useful.

After arriving at a feasible subject, an exposition using this subject should be written. Again, experimentation will pay off.

  1) Different arrangements of entrances in the exposition should be tried. Sometimes a subject will work better, for example, as a middle voice than it will as an upper voice in the first statement of an exposition.

  2) Writing the exposition will involve writing the response, a countersubject, and the full three-voice setting of the third entrance. In the countersubject, experimentation with different lines to find the one which sounds best and can do the most in possible later development is recommended.

When the exposition is settled on, planning is necessary, at least roughly, to determine what will happen in the rest of the fugue.

  1) In the previous experimentation, and in further experiments, the possible devices which can satisfactorily be used should be well proved. These should be divided among the sections of the fugue so that there is a balance and a degree of progressive difficulty.

  2) Assuming a three-section form as a basic structure, the first section can be planned as involving the simpler devices of imitation — sequence, fragmentation, inversion, and combinations of these. Of course, these simple devices are the heart of *all* contrapuntal development, and will be found throughout the fugue.

  3) The second section should perhaps contain two-voice strettos, shifted rhythm, statements on different scale steps, and perhaps the three-voice stretto, in addition to the further use of the simple devices.

     a) Two-voice strettos with a third voice moving freely are fairly easy to come by. Two of them at different time intervals, using the first and second, and first and third, voices of the three-voice stretto, may be extracted from the original three-voice stretto.

     b) The three-voice stretto will appear in the second section only if there is enough material remaining to make a third section interesting. Otherwise, the three-voice stretto should be saved for the third section.

  4) In the third section, the most complicated devices should appear.

     a) At least one augmentation with two statements appearing against it should be used here. Often this is a good device, with its effect of broadening, to lead into the final cadence.

     b) If the three-voice stretto has not been used, it should appear here. If it is found that this stretto will work with voices inverted, or in different voice arrangements, it may be possible to use different versions in both sections.

     c) It is quite common for a fugue to end with a codetta, usually following a deceptive cadence. This will often contain a final statement of the subject.

  5) In general, the following devices can be used throughout the fugue:

     a) Statements on different scale steps, often at the beginning of a section.

     b) New counterpoints which may develop into useful episodic material.

     c) All of the simple contrapuntal devices.

6) It should be kept in mind that in episodic passages, changes may be made in the material quite freely in order to make it do some of the things which seem necessary.

   a) It is very common for the size and quality of intervals to be changed as necessary adjustments in some of the more complicated devices.
   b) Notes may be interpolated in the original material, or notes may be left out.
   c) Strict handling is necessary only for the exposition and the three-voice stretto. Part of the three-voice stretto may be omitted if it does not work.
   d) The only guide is that the more closely the original material is adhered to, the more coherent the manipulations will be. The only element of unity or continuity in a fugue is the use of common material. If this is changed to the point that it cannot be recognized, the purpose has been defeated and the fugue fails as a coherent piece of music.

7) A good device is the use of the longer rest occasionally to give a contrast of texture and "breathing" space. A rest of any length should never be used to avoid a problem. Side-stepping the issue in such a way is usually very obvious. The use of the rest should have musically artistic justification. The use of rests to emphasize the entrance of important devices must be remembered as a valuable tool.

8) It is possible to use other forms than the three-section form. Any pattern of sections which can be validated as having balance, unity, and contrast, and which gives the opportunity for harmonic contrasts, is acceptable.

Assignments

1) Produce a subject by writing a three-voice stretto as described in this Chapter, and use it as the basis for a full three-voice fugue.
2) Extend one or more of the expositions completed for Chapter 27 into a full three-voice fugue according to the directions above if it is found that the subject will work in three-voice stretto.

The Well-Tempered Clavier is the highest and best school; no one will ever create a more ideal one.

—Chopin

Part V

Chapter 30

The Association of Four Voices

Counterpoint in four voices has very little new to offer over the now familiar three-voice counterpoint. There are an increase in the density of the texture and added possibilities for achieving variety, both in texture and in the manipulation of materials.

All that has been said in Chapter 19, The Association of Three Voices, and practiced in the ensuing Chapters is still valid in respect to counterpoint in four, or even more, voices. Chapter 19 should be reviewed thoroughly. Certain expansions and modifications of the statements found there are all that is required.

MELODIC MOVEMENT

For convenience, the designation of voices in four-voice counterpoint will be adopted from vocal style, although the immediate concern is with the instrumental idiom.

1) The Soprano (S), Alto (A), Tenor (T), and Bass (B) voices will have the following ranges in this style:

EXAMPLE 157

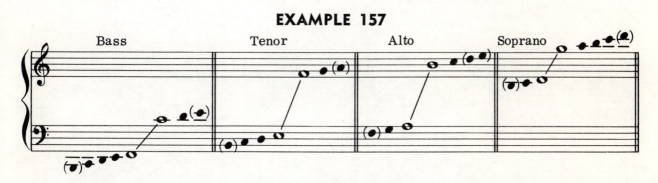

2) Because four voices are now used where there formerly were three, the tessitura (range) of the individual voices will be somewhat smaller.

3) The ranges as shown above are approximations. No voice should be used at either extreme of its range for very long, and the voice should turn back as soon as is practical. Exceeding the best, or normal, range for very long causes a voice to lose its character or identity. This is especially true in music written for a keyboard instrument.

The strong harmonic tendency of a four-voice texture makes it even more imperative that individual melodic lines be clear and logical in their movements so that the ear may be drawn to them instead of to the strong vertical combinations.

1) Stepwise melodic movement should predominate, since too many strong skips and leaps only compound the problem of the inherent harmonic strength of the texture.
2) The stronger non-chord tones (neighboring tone, escape tone, and appoggiatura) are more practical than before because the desired harmony can be strong enough in the remaining voices to make their meaning clear. They have less tendency to disturb the intended harmonic implication, and, in fact, aid in concealing it.
3) Occasionally, for short periods of time, overlapping, and even direct crossing, of voices may be effective, or thematically necessary. This practice must not be used to the extent that it permanently dislocates the proper relationship of voices.

EXAMPLE 158

Ties and syncopations are used very freely as a means of concealing the harmony, and as an aid in maintaining the independence of the voices.

1) Ties of longer duration are found more frequently than in three-voice texture.
2) More than one voice may be found tied at the same time. The only restriction in this case is that one voice must move on the beat in order that the metric definition will not be lost.
3) An extended tie may become a pedal point. This will usually occur in the bass voice, but may occur in any voice. Pedal points are much more effective in four voices than they were in three, since the desired harmony can be more firmly defined in the remaining three voices. (See Chapter 19, page 89.)

EXAMPLE 159

(Suspended V^7/V)

(V) ——————— V

RHYTHMIC MOVEMENT

It is characteristic of contrapuntal writing that the thicker the texture (the more voices that are introduced), the slower the basic rhythmic movement will become. This has stylistic as well as practical application in that a more complicated texture becomes more difficult to play, and more difficult for the listener to comprehend.

The basic rhythmic movement of a four-voice texture will seldom exceed eighth notes, and often will be in quarter notes, or sometimes, even in half notes in *alla breve* meter. Faster note values occur, but may not be used often enough, nor consistently enough to become the basic rhythmic pulse (Fugue XVIII). Frequent exceptions to this slower basic rhythmic movement are usually based on the fact that a voice is omitted often enough that the piece will really fall under the principles of three-voice writing, where faster movement is more feasible (Fugue XVII).

The balance of rhythmic movement between the four voices is achieved in the same manner as before.

1) The use of four voices makes it more possible to use parallel rhythmic patterns in pairs of voices, alternating frequently.
2) The rhythmic movement should not become too complicated. If it does, it can lead to confusion instead of rhythmic strength. Judicious use of the longer ties to sustain one voice (or more) will help in easing the complication.
3) Parallel thirds and sixths in connection with parallel rhythmic movement is still a useful device, and is handled the same as in three voices.

Rests are found to have a new, important application in a four-voice texture.

1) The *short* rests are still used in the same manner as in three voices, mainly to emphasize a thematic entrance by delay.
2) The *longer* rests are frequent, their application being the same as in three voices.
3) In four-voice texture, it is frequent to find *extended* rests of several measures' duration.

   a) The result of the use of this type of rest is to reduce the texture to three, or sometimes two, voices for purposes of contrast, and to avoid becoming too thick and heavy.
   b) The extended rest should not be used to avoid the difficulties of writing four-voice counterpoint, however. Its purpose is an artistic one, and its use should be so governed.

HARMONIC CONTENT

Three voices are all that are needed to imply very definitely all the harmonic vocabulary of the early eighteenth century. Even the dominant seventh chord, and other seventh chords sometimes encountered can be defined very adequately in only three voices. The fourth voice, then, has the effect of reinforcing the implied harmony by doublings, thus thickening and strengthening the harmonic structure. The tendency of four-voice counterpoint to gravitate toward the inherently stronger harmonic element is one of the main concerns in writing in this idiom.

1) The basic harmonic movement needs to be especially clear and natural, and relatively uncomplicated.

2) All that has been said concerning the lowest (Bass) voice, and the handling of six-four chord implications in three voices (Chapter 19, page 92.) is doubly important in four voices.

3) The question of doubling which arises in a four-voice texture with triads as the basic harmonic material may best be clarified thus:

    a) Any doubling which occurs in opposition to the general rules of part-writing as laid down in the study of traditional harmonic practices must be justified either in that it be understood as being necessary to the logical conduct of the individual voices involved in the doubling, or that it be the result of the use of some important device of thematic development.

    b) Doubling of non-chord tones is frequent, and will be judged mainly on the logical progression of the lines involved. Any exceptional doublings should be avoided on strong parts of beats.

    c) The best general rule for doubling is the application of musical logic. If all elements make good musical sense, then it is feasible to allow occasional exceptional doublings.

THEMATIC CONSIDERATIONS

Characteristic treatment of material in four voices is aimed mainly at three points:

1) Maintaining melodic independence of the voices.
2) Suppressing the inherent harmonic strength of the four-voice texture.
3) Avoiding excess complication of melodic and rhythmic textures to keep the result from sounding overloaded or confused.

In order to maintain a balance of voices, no melodic or rhythmic relationship should be continued for more than two or three beats.

One important device for maintaining equality of voices is that of "fragmentary imitation." This is the use of short melodic rhythmic figures imitated in all the voices. These short imitations will move from voice to voice in irregular order, need not be strict, and sometimes are only hinted at. (See three-voice Example 124, Chapter 20.)

The natural weight of the lower pitches common to the bass register tends to slow the movement in the lowest voice. Special attention needs to be paid that this voice share equally in the melodic and rhythmic movement so that it will not become forgotten and degenerate into a bass-line accompaniment.

It is generally said that four-voice (or more) textures lead to a more profound, serious style in the music. This is due to the increased complication of the musical content. This characteristic is sometimes shown in the use of slower note values, but just as often, it is the result of a slower tempo adopted by the player to clarify the performance.

It should be remembered that Maelzel did not produce the metronome until 1816, so Bach had no way of making precise indications of tempi. These were set by custom and the style and texture of the music itself. It is generally accepted that Bach's intended tempi were markedly slower than many performers demonstrate today.

Study Questions

1) What is gained by the use of a four-voice texture?
2) What are the normal ranges of the four voices?
3) What is the general rule for exceeding this normal range?
4) Why is it possible to use the neighboring tone and the escape tone more effectively now?
5) What added freedom is available in the use of ties in four voices? What is the purpose of tied notes?
6) Discuss the rhythmic movement of a four-voice texture.
7) Name the three types of rests, and describe the best use of each.
8) What are the main points for consideration in the treatment of thematic material in four voices?

Harmonic Analysis

Analyze harmonically the following four-voice excerpts from Book I, *Well-Tempered Clavier* with chord numerals for the basic harmonic background, and non-chord tone symbols. Some of these excerpts do not lie within the original key, some may modulate, and some may have added voices near the end.

Fugue	I	— last seven measures and two beats
Prelude	VII	— last eight measures and two beats
Fugue	XII	— measure 27, third beat, to measure 30, third beat
Fugue	XIV	— measure 32, to end
Fugue	XVI	— measure 14, third beat, to measure 18, third beat
Fugue	XVIII	— measure 32, third beat to end
Fugue	XX	— measure 24, third beat, to measure 27, third beat

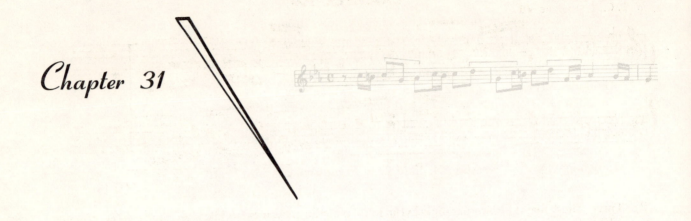

Chapter 31

Four-Voice Writing – A

All of the principles stated in Chapter 20 concerning three-voice writing are still valid for four voices. The "basic rhythm" of four voices may be slower than that specified for three voices. (See Chapter 30, page 143.) The use of faster note values (sixteenths) is very common, but they will generally be used to vary or ornament a basic slower-moving pattern.

W. T. C.   I,   Fugue   I,   measures 17 and 18

The difficulty of maintaining four interesting lines is obvious.

1) Often the four voices may "pair off" in terms of melodic or rhythmic movement with this "pairing" being shifted frequently.

EXAMPLE 160

W. T. C. I, Prelude VII

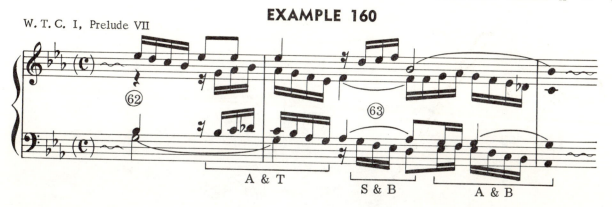

2) Three voices may fall into parallel rhythmic or melodic movement while the fourth voice remains relatively stationary, possibly as a pedal point.

EXAMPLE 161

W. T. C. I, Fugue XX

3) Two voices may carry on independently, either in imitation or in parallel movement, with the other two becoming relatively unimportant for a short time.

W. T. C. I, Fugue XII

EXAMPLE 162

4) Occasionally it will be found that one voice may have the leading activity by itself with the other three subordinated to it. The other voices may be in slower movement, perhaps even parallel, or one or more may be sustained.

EXAMPLE 163

(See also Fugue XVII, measure 30 to end.)

5) As was stated in Chapter 30, page 144. (and shown in Example 124, Chapter 20), imitation of short figures, "fragmentary imitation," involving all of the voices, or most of them, is an excellent device for maintaining the relative importance of all the voices.

6) None of these movements can be used for too long a time because a voice can become "lost" much more quickly in four voices than in three.

The harmonic significance of the vertical combinations must be kept in mind, and careful attention paid to the implied harmonies and their progression. Again, these harmonies must be concealed by intelligent use of non-chord tones. Harmonic content should be simple, and its movement relatively slow.

One practical approach to the writing of a four-voice texture is that of beginning with two voices combined according to the rules of two-voice writing and adding two more voices in the same, or a compatible, style.

1) The two added voices should take their characteristic rhythm and melodic movement (style) from the two given voices as much as is practical.

2) They should complete and double the harmonic background implied by the two given voices.

3) A certain amount of parallel movement, rhythmically and harmonically, with the given lines will lend unity to the whole.

4) The given voices *may not be the same voices throughout the exercise;* hence the direction of note stems must be carefully observed.

5) Too much movement should be avoided. Occasional longer ties will be allowed if needed.

6) Opportunities for the use of fragmentary imitation should be sought out.

7) The results of experiments in writing four-voice counterpoint in this manner should be examined for the following points:

a) The total rhythm should be even and there should be no dead spots except possibly occurring on strong beats of the measure.

b) Each line, independently tested, should make melodic sense, and the tendency of all active tones should be fulfilled.

c) The harmony must be clear, must progress logically, and must not be too strongly implied. (Does it sound too much like a chorale?)

d) There must be unity of style, and all voices must share in melodic and rhythmic interest.

Exercises in Completing Two-Voice Sketches

Complete the following sketches in four voices according to the principles stated.

MODEL 6

EXERCISE 22

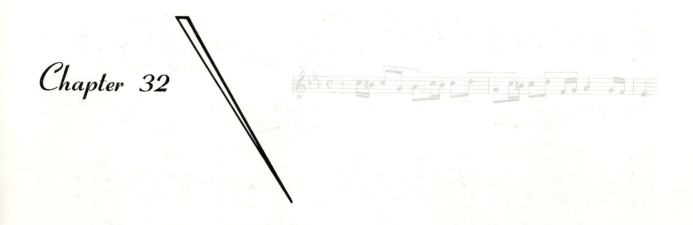

Chapter 32

Four-Voice Writing – B

Two other practical approaches to writing four-voice counterpoint are that of building up a four-voice texture from a single given line and that of writing four lines to elaborate and ornament a harmonic progression.

The first approach would occur when one line is found to be carrying the important thread of thematic development and the other three need to be added to it.

1) The harmonic implications inherent in the single given line need to be determined, and the other three lines added in such a way as to help define the necessary harmonies.
2) The added lines may take their style from that of the given line.
3) It is possible that tasteful contrasts, rhythmic and melodic, may be introduced in the added lines.
4) Devices for unity of style already mentioned should be introduced as needed.
5) The added lines must join with the given line to form a unified whole.
6) It is best to work one line at a time, but for no more than a beat or two, and then bring the other lines up to it. A single line should not be carried all the way through or the equality of voices will suffer.
7) The four-voice result should be checked in the same manner as in the previous Chapter.

Exercises

Add three voices to the given line:

MODEL 7

(Thematic line)

EXERCISE 23

The second approach, that of ornamenting a harmonic progression, would become necessary if a certain harmonic progression is to be the most important feature, as at points of cadence or if certain necessary modulations need to be accomplished. In these exercises, it will be necessary to pay special attention to the matter of style, since there is no rhythmic guide given.

1) The ornamentation of the individual lines of the given progression should be accomplished by the introduction of non-chord tones, as well as other tones of the momentary chord, and short rests, to produce a free, interesting melodic flow in each voice.
2) The problem of concealing the harmony is foremost.
3) Again, no one voice should be carried forward for more than a beat or two without filling out the texture in order that all voices be given equal consideration.
4) All devices used to obtain unity of style and melodic independence, as well as rhythmic unity, need to be used.
5) The four-voice result should be checked in the manner of the foregoing exercises.

Exercises

Elaboration of harmonic sketches:

MODEL 8

Harmonic Sketch:

I °VII$^6_5$ I^6 °II VI$^6_4$ °II^7 °VII$^6_5$ V^7 I

Elaboration:

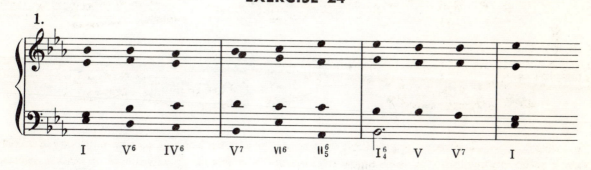

EXERCISE 24

1.

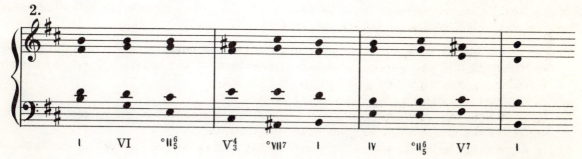

I V^6 IV^6 V^7 VI^6 II$^6_5$ I$^6_4$ V V^7 I

2.

I VI °II$^6_5$ V$^4_3$ °VII^7 I IV °II$^6_5$ V^7 I

3.

I I$^6_4$ IV^6 °II$^6_5$ V^7 VI +III^6 I$^6_4$ IV^6 I^6 °II$^6_5$ V^7 I

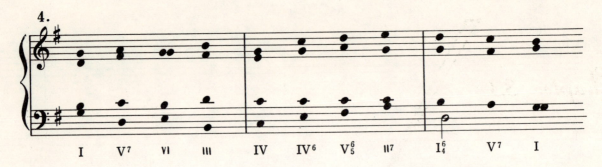

4.

I   V⁷   VI   III   IV   IV⁶   V⁶₅   II⁷   I⁶₄   V⁷   I

No one method of approach to four-voice writing will be found to be the total answer. Differing situations in the course of writing will call for a particular approach, and each should be used as needed. While some students may find one approach easier than another, all methods will be found to have equal value in the total result.

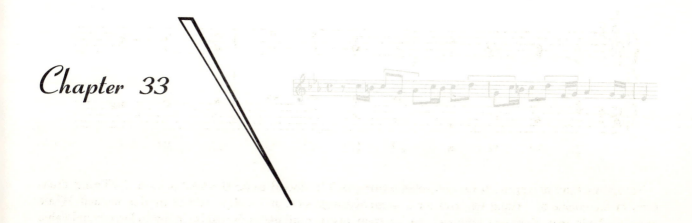

Chapter 33

The Four-Voice Fugue – A

In structure and principle, the four-voice fugue parallels the three-voice fugue as described in Chapters 25 through 28. The only added problems are those of introducing the fourth voice, and of tastefully handling the more complicated texture.

THE EXPOSITION

The function of the exposition is, as before, (1) to introduce the thematic material (subject) in each voice, (2) to present a suitable and useful countersubject, and (3) to add other, less important, counterpoints to these lines to form a four-voice texture, stressing the tonic key.

The subject of a four-voice fugue does not differ in any appreciable respect from that found in the three-voice fugues (Chapter 25).

1) Longer, slower-moving subjects may be found in Bach's four-voice Fugues, but no more frequently than in his Fugues in three voices. Influencing the rhythmic movement of the subject is the amount of actual four-voice texture intended to be used in episodes, slower movement lending itself more readily to extensive four-voice treatment without the danger of overloading.

2) The subject is still a complete musical thought, a phrase or sometimes a period in length, ending with a rather definite cadence on a strong beat.

3) The subject is stated alone, *usually in either the Tenor or the Alto voice.*

   a) Occasionally, the initial statement of the subject is in the Bass voice (Fugue V, and also five-voice Fugue IV).

   b) Very rarely the first statement could appear in the Soprano, but this highest entrance is usually reserved for a later statement to add shape to the exposition, serving, in effect, as a kind of climax.

The response (second entrance) is governed by the same principles as that of the three-voice fugue (Chapter 26).

1) The response appears as an imitation at the fifth from the initial statement.
2) It occurs in an *adjacent* voice to the subject.
3) All principles governing the use of the tonal response are exactly the same as in the three-voice fugue, and must be observed.

The countersubject, which is the continuation of the line which first announced the subject and which serves as a counterpoint to the response, has the same function and characteristics as it had in the three-voice fugue (Chapter 27).

1) Its main functions are to provide some melodic and rhythmic interest or contrast, and to help confirm the harmonic implications of the response.

2) Sometimes the countersubject is conceived as a true contrapuntal associate, and as such will reappear repeatedly with the subject in later use, either as a whole or in part.

The melodic bridge following the response and adjusting the harmony to allow the third entrance of the subject to appear as a tonic entrance, is used in the same way as before, and is just as essential (Chapter 27).

The remaining two entrances of the subject material needed to complete the exposition by introducing the other two voices of the four-voice fugue do not conform to a set pattern often enough for definite statements to be made about their order of entrance.

1) The third entrance appears as another statement of the subject (in the tonic) an octave removed from the first statement. A rare exception is seen in Fugue I of the *Well-Tempered Clavier*, Book I, in which the third entrance is another dominant, or response, version of the subject. This may have been experimental on Bach's part, since this is the only example of such an entrance in the two books of the *Well-Tempered Clavier.*

2) The fourth entrance appears as another response (at the fifth), and is an octave removed from the second statement. This will give the typical exposition of a four-voice fugue the pattern of Subject (Tonic), Response (Dominant), Subject (Tonic), Response (Dominant).

   Exceptions to this order may be found in Fugues XII and XIV of Book 1, where the fourth voice appears as another subject (in the tonic). In both of these cases, the third and fourth entrances are separated by a three-voice bridge so extensive as to appear almost as a misplaced episode. It is tempting to analyze these cases as exceptional three-voice expositions, but the ensuing four-voice texture requires that the fourth entrance appear to complete the exposition.

3) The order of voices for the third and fourth entrances can best be determined by examination of the Fugues of Bach as seen in the *Well-Tempered Clavier.* The following table shows the order of entrances in the nineteen four-voice Fugues found in both books of the *Well-Tempered Clavier* and the frequency with which they appear.

Order of Voices	Number of times used
T　A　S　B	4
B　T　A　S	4
A　S　T　B	3
A　S　B　T	3
A　T　B　S	2
T　A　B　S	2
T　B　S　A	1

⌒ – indicates adjacent voices

⌒‸ – indicates skip of one voice

⌒‸‸ – indicates skip of two voices

a) The choice of order seems to be dictated by several factors, mainly range (placement on the staff), voicing of the harmony at the point of entrance, and artistic balance, or shape, of the exposition as a whole. The six-four chord should be avoided at the entrance of a new voice.

b) It may be necessary to try a subject in several different arrangements until all these factors are properly adjusted.

There are instances in which a melodic bridge appears between the third and fourth entrances, but this cannot be said to be common practice. (See Fugue XXIV, Book I, measure 12.) The appearance of such a bridge might be explained in one of two ways:

1) The harmony or voicing might be such at the end of the third statement that an immediate entrance in the fourth voice would seem awkward.
2) The composer might consider a bridge at this point necessary for artistic reasons, such as balance, contrast, or dramatic effect.

The exposition ends in either dominant or tonic harmony on a strong beat. Seldom will any other harmony appear at this point. The choice of chord is dictated by the type of response used.

1) In the four-voice fugues, the end of the exposition may be rather indefinite harmonically, making a smooth elision into the first episode.
2) If the cadence is too well concealed, the use of obvious devices of development will indicate that the episode has begun.
3) The *extra* entrance, sometimes noted in the expositions of three-voice fugues (Chapter 27, page 132.), is not found in the four-voice fugues. Occasionally a restatement of the subject near the beginning of the first episode may appear to be a "fifth entrance," but harmonic analysis will show that it does not hold to the tonic well enough to be included in the exposition but is really a part of the episodic development.

The added voices appearing with the third and fourth entrances to complete the texture are not usually very significant.

1) If lines are written which will supply new material for possible later use, this is of course all to the good.
2) Often these lines are so ordinary (especially the last line to be added) as to be almost useless for later development.
3) For analysis, the symbol ∧∧∧ may be used to indicate the new material appearing with the fourth entrance.

Analysis of Expositions

Analyze the expositions of the four-voice Fugues contained in the *Well-Tempered Clavier,* Book I. These Fugues are I, V, XII, XIV, XVI, XVII, XVIII, XX, XXIII, and XXIV. Use the diagram form of analysis, noting carefully the following points:

1) Characteristics of the subject.
2) Type of response.
3) The use of a melodic bridge, and its source.
4) The order of entrances.
5) Relationship of the auxiliary lines to one another as they appear with each statement.
6) Any exceptional elements which may appear.

Study Questions

1) Compare the subject normally found in a four-voice fugue with that used in a three-voice fugue.
2) What element may influence the rhythmic movement of the subject?
3) Which voice first states the subject, and how?

4) What principles govern the response? In which voice will it appear?
5) Discuss the countersubject.
6) How is the melodic bridge used, and when?
7) Discuss the two remaining entrances as to form and order of succession.
8) How should the exposition end?
9) Discuss the counterpoints to the third and fourth entrances.

Assignments

1) Write four-voice expositions according to the principles found in this Chapter, and in the analysis, using several of the following subjects.

EXERCISE 25

2) Write original subjects patterned after the style of the subjects found in the *Well-Tempered Clavier,* and continue into complete four-voice expositions.

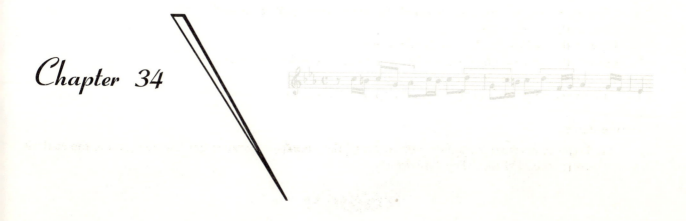

Chapter 34

The Four-Voice Fugue – B

The remaining sections of the fugue will follow the same general pattern of organization as was found in the three-voice fugues. Sectional form is again the one most commonly found. More extended forms are usually expansions or elaborations of simpler forms. The important factor to remember is that the purpose of form in music is to give a feeling of balance and organization to the development of musical ideas.

CONTRAPUNTAL MANIPULATION

All devices of contrapuntal manipulation previously used can be found in the episodes of four-voice fugues, but it is noticeable that four-voice texture does not lend itself well to the use of complicated devices. The simpler devices are found to predominate.

1) Restatements of the subject, both as a whole and in part, are very common in episodes and they may appear on any scale steps.

   a) These restatements sometimes follow each other two or three at a time, or,
   b) They may appear alternating with short episodic passages.
   c) Such restatements are particularly useful in the development of a slow-moving subject (Fugue XII, Book I).

2) The stretto is less useful, except for the two-voice stretto, often used in a pair of voices imitating another pair.

EXAMPLE 164

W. T. C. I, Fugue I

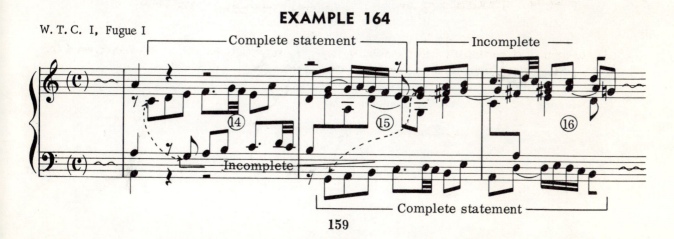

a) There are rare appearances of the three-voice stretto, but often in a rather incomplete manner.

EXAMPLE 165

W. T. C. I, Fugue XVI

b) The four-voice stretto is best not attempted. A line which can be made to work in a four-voice stretto would no doubt make a very unexpressive subject.

c) Stretto development is successful only when the subject has enough movement near its beginning to make it recognizable before the entry of the next voice. This means that a slow-moving subject will probably not make a good stretto, especially in a four-voice texture. (See the confusion resulting in the stretto attempts in five-voice Fugue XXII, beginning with the last half of measure 67.)

d) The best practice is to make certain that the subject chosen will produce at least a partial two-voice stretto of good quality.

It would seem that augmentation and diminution would be useful, but actual examples of these in the four-voice Fugues of the *Well-Tempered* are very rare.

Natural double counterpoint is very useful in pairs of voices, and should be planned.

A very useful, and necessary, device is that of omitting one voice in episodic sections, thereby producing a temporary three-voice texture. In addition to providing an often welcome contrast to the density of four voices, this will allow many devices of manipulation to be heard more distinctly. A voice may be omitted in an episode for several beats, or even for several measures.

1) This is common practice in the four-voice Fugues of Bach, and is to be recommended.
2) The voice omitted will stop at a relatively strong rhythmic point on a tone which has no active feeling or need for resolution.
3) When this voice returns, it will best have some thematically important idea, usually entering after a short rest.
4) The following examples should be studied for the use of three-voice texture in four-voice fugues:

From Book I of the *Well-Tempered Clavier*

Fugue I   — measure 7 to first beat of measure 12
Fugue XII   — measure 16 to fourth beat of measure 27
Fugue XIV   — measure 18 to measure 32
Fugue XVI   — measure 18 to measure 29
Fugue XVII   — measure 19 to measure 29
Fugue XVIII — measure 28 to third beat of measure 32
Fugue XX   — measure 18 to measure 21

It is even possible, for shorter periods of time, to reduce the texture to two voices. This will happen only after a strong cadence (at the beginning of a section).

1) Two-voice texture must be used only with some important device, such as a stretto, which needs utmost clarity.

2) It should not last for more than three or four beats.
3) See the following examples of the use of two-voice texture:

From Book I of the *Well-Tempered Clavier*

Fugue I   — measure 14
Fugue XIV   — measure 28
Fugue XVII   — measures 16 and 23
Fugue XX   — measures 65 through 67

Analysis

Analyze several of the four-voice Fugues in chart form, paying special attention to means of development used in episodes, and the forms into which the Fugues resolve themselves.

Study Questions

1) What form is found in the four-voice Fugues?
2) How are more extended forms arrived at?
3) What devices of contrapuntal manipulation are commonly used?
4) What is the usefulness of the stretto in relation to the four-voice Fugues?
5) What is "change of texture"? How, and why, is this accomplished?

Writing a Four-Voice Fugue

1) Extend one of the expositions for Chapter 33 into a full four-voice fugue.
2) Write a four-voice fugue on an original subject.

a) Produce the subject in the manner of the subjects for the three-voice fugues in Chapter 29.

b) The stretto possibilities need not be carried out as completely as for the subject of the three-voice fugues, but the more adaptable the subject is to stretto manipulation, the more valuable it will be. A significant amount of the subject — enough to be recognizable — should lend itself to stretto imitation, and in three voices if possible.

c) Use the analysis of Bach's Fugues as guides, and make frequent reference to the Fugues of Bach for answers to questions of form, manipulation, and sequence of material.

Appendix A

Terminology of harmonic structures and functions as presented in most courses in traditional harmony depends greatly on the individual teacher's background and personal concepts. The furor often encountered in discussion of conflicting terminologies is meaningless. The actual names of harmonic elements under discussion are only tools to be used to arrive at a common understanding for clarity in talking about the music at hand. Teachers use terms with which they were trained, or, in the case of thinking teachers, modifications, or clarifications of these. The music itself exists and endures in spite of the varied names applied to its sometimes insignificant elements.

It is necessary, however, for a group to come to a common understanding in order that classes not become a veritable "Tower of Babel." The keynote is clarity and simplicity for ease of use.

It is for this reason that the following presentation is made. Agreement or disagreement notwithstanding, the following system of terminologies is used in this text.

DIATONIC CHORD IDENTIFICATION

The system of using large (capital) and small (lower case) Roman numerals provides an accurate indication of the quality of the chord identified, and requires the student to be *aware* of the kind of material he is handling, which, in many cases, is important to the manner in which he handles it.

1) The *size* of the numeral indicates the quality of the *third* of the chord. Thus, a *large* numeral (I) indicates a *major third* in the chord, while a *small* numeral (i) shows that the *third of the chord is minor* in quality.

2) If there is no other indication, then the *fifth* of the chord is assumed to be *perfect*.

3) In the case of chords containing augmented or diminished fifths, the symbol $^+$ for "augmented," or $^\circ$ for "diminished" is added *before* the chord numeral, thus:

$$^+\text{III} \quad - \text{ augmented three chord}$$
$$^\circ\text{vii} \quad - \text{ diminished seven chord}$$

The reason for adding the symbol *before* the chord numeral (contrary to the practice of a number of harmony texts) is simply that this is the way the chord is "spoken," with the qualifying term *preceding* the name of the chord. Also, the symbol in this location does not become so easily confused with the figures added to indicate inversions of these chords.

4) Dissonant harmonies involving sevenths are indicated by the addition of the figure 7 following the proper sized chord numeral:

V^7 — five-seven chord
$^{\circ}vii^7$ — diminished seven-seven chord
ii^7 — two-seven chord

In diatonic harmonies, the seventh takes its spelling from the scale, and its quality is not critical. The $^{\circ}vii^7$ in minor has a diminished seventh, and so, in root position, *may* be indicated thus: $^{\circ}vii^{\circ 7}$.

$I^{\,6}_{\,4}$ — one-six-four chord

$^{\circ}ii^{\,4}_{\,3}$ — diminished two-four-three chord

There is no need to clutter up this figuration with accidentals to indicate the raised leading tone in a minor key, such as $V^{\#6}_{\ \ 3}$, or $V^7_{\#}$, or the varied versions of this appearing in some theory texts, since the large-sized numeral indicates that the chord is major, and the only way it can be major, in diatonic harmony, is for its third (which is the leading tone) to be raised.

FUNCTIONAL IDENTIFICATION

Altered chords found within traditional harmony are altered, not to make life miserable for theory students, but to lend these chords new identity, or function within the harmonic scheme. In the music of Bach, we may say for practical purposes that the only useful altered chord found (other than those "borrowed" alterations derived from the use of the melodic minor scale) is the *secondary* (or "applied") *dominant*.

1) The secondary dominant chord is a chord which has been altered by the *addition of one or more accidentals* so that it assumes the *form* and temporary *function* of a dominant chord to a diatonic chord other than the tonic.

2) Chords intended to perform this function will be altered to assume one of these forms:

a)  A chord of dominant seventh structure, containing a major third, a perfect fifth, and a minor seventh.

b)  A major triad with major third and perfect fifth, duplicating the structure of a dominant triad.

c)  A diminished chord, containing a minor third, a diminished fifth, and a minor seventh (half-diminished seventh chord) duplicating the structure of the $^{\circ}vii^7$ in a major key, or a diminished seventh (fully-diminished seventh chord) duplicating the structure of the $^{\circ}vii^{\circ 7}$ in a minor key.

d)  A diminished triad, with minor third and diminished fifth, duplicating the structure of the leading tone triad ($^{\circ}vii$).

3) These chords so altered will have the same root relationship and tendency for resolution to a diatonic chord as the V⁷, V, °vii⁷, or °vii to their tonic.

EXAMPLE 166

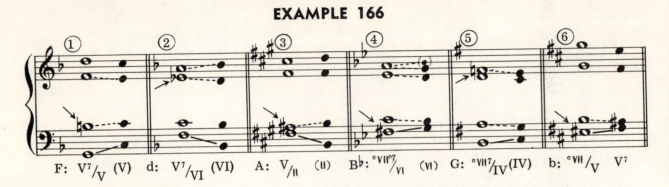

F: V⁷/V (V)   d: V⁷/VI (VI)   A: V/II   (II)   B♭: °VII°⁷/VI   (VI)   G: °VII⁷/IV (IV)   b: °VII/V   V⁷

a) Chords assuming V⁷, or V, structure will have roots which lie a perfect fourth below the root of the chord to which they are being applied. (See Example 166, 1, 2, and 3.)

b) Chords assuming °vii⁷, or °vii, structure will have roots related as temporary leading tones to the root of the chord to which they are being applied. (See Example 166, 4, 5, and 6.)

(1) Note that in Example 166, 4, the secondary dominant is constructed to resolve to a minor chord (vi) which, as a temporary tonic, suggests that the secondary dominant contain a diminished seventh, peculiar to the °vii⁷ in a minor key.

(2) In Example 166, 5, the secondary dominant is constructed to resolve to a major triad (IV), so the seventh in the secondary dominant is minor, a characteristic of the °vii⁷ in a major key.

c) The symbols for identification used in Example 166 above are a convenient way of expressing the structure of the chord, and its relationship to the key.

d) All inversions are practical in the use of these chords, and all rules of resolution for the V, V⁷, °vii⁷, and °vii, should be adhered to.

e) It is feasible that a secondary dominant may appear in a *deceptive* resolution (parallel to the resolution of the V⁷ or °vii⁷ to vi instead of to the tonic). They will resolve to the chord with root a third lower than the one to which they were constructed.

EXAMPLE 167

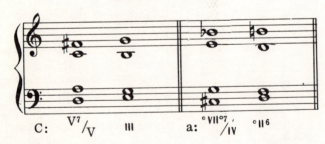

C: V⁷/V   III   a: °VII°⁷/IV   °II⁶

4) The use of these secondary dominant chords simplifies the problems of analysis by making it possible to eliminate the so-called "transient" modulations, allowing modulation to be applied only when a *definite* change of key has been accomplished. In order to be considered completed, a change of key must have a minimum of three chords in the new key *after* the point of modulation (common chord).

NON-CHORD TONES

The following is a listing of terminologies and definitions of non-chord tones as used in this text and an attempt to correlate them with other terminologies in common use. Of the six theory texts chosen to be used as points of comparison, five are in extensive use in colleges throughout the country. The sixth, Goetchius, was chosen because he can be said to be the "father of us all" regardless of how far removed we may seem to have become.

The texts are referred to only as they present some *differing* terminology, or approach, to the presentation in this text. The complete list of texts used follows:

> Forte, Allen, *Tonal Harmony in Concept and Practice*
> Goetschius, Percy, *Material Used in Musical Composition*
> Hindemith, Paul, *Traditional Harmony*, Book I, rev. ed.
> McHose, Allen Irvine, *The Contrapuntal Harmonic Techniques of the Eighteenth Century*
> Ottman, Robert W., *Elementary Harmony; Advanced Harmony*
> Piston, Walter, *Harmony*, third ed.

1) PASSING TONE — (P)

EXAMPLE 168

(chromatic)

Approached and left by step in the same direction, along the scale line, filling the interval between two chord tones. May appear on either strong or weak beats, or parts of beats.

Forte:	"pn" — "passing note"
Goetschius:	"x" — accented; "+" — unaccented
Ottman:	"UPT" — unaccented; "APT" — accented
Piston:	"p.t." — unaccented only (accented is classed as an appoggiatura)

2) AUXILIARY — (N̶)

EXAMPLE 169

Approached and left by step in opposite directions, returning to the chord tone from which it started. May appear on either strong or weak beats, or parts of beats. Lower auxiliary may be raised if it lies a major second from the principal tone.

Forte:	"aux" — "complete auxiliary note"
Goetschius:	"o" — "neighboring note" ("embellishment")
Hindemith:	"changing tone"
McHose:	"neighboring note"
Ottman:	"UN" — "upper neighboring tone"
	"LN" — "lower neighboring tone"
Piston:	"aux"

a) DOUBLE AUXILIARY (N̶N̶)

EXAMPLE 170

Simplified from:

Moves in pattern of step — skip in opposite direction — step, back to beginning tone. May move in either direction. Rhythmic placement may be shifted. Figure may be inverted.

Forte: included in "complete auxiliary note"
Hindemith: "neighboring tone" (covered by definition)
McHose: "changing tones"
Ottman: "CT" — "changing tones"
Piston: "camb." — "cambiata" (no approach discussed)

b) CAMBIATA (N̶N̶)

EXAMPLE 171

Beginning with chord tone, down a step, down a third, up a step to a chord tone. Like double auxiliary except for substitution of another chord tone for the first tone of the pattern. May be inverted. Rhythmic placement may be shifted, which may displace non-chord tones.

Hindemith: see "double auxiliary" above
Piston: see "double auxiliary" above

3) SUSPENSION — (S)

EXAMPLE 172

Approached by being held over or repeated from a tone of the preceding chord, and left by step. Appears on strong beat, or strong part of beat.

McHose: refers to suspension resolving upward as "retardation"
Ottman: see McHose — "R" — "retardation"
Piston: "susp."

4) ANTICIPATION — (A)

EXAMPLE 173

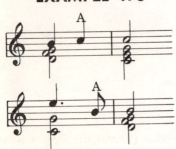

Approached from a chord tone by step or leap, repeated (or tied) to a tone of the next chord. Appears on weak beat, or weak part of beat.

McHose: approach only by step
Ottman: see McHose
Piston: "ant."

5) APPOGGIATURA — (Ap)

EXAMPLE 174

Approached by skip or leap, left by step, appearing on strong beat, or strong part of beat. Step best in opposite direction from approach.

Forte:	"incomplete auxiliary note" ("prefix" type)
Goetschius:	"o" — irregular neighbor note
Hindemith:	"neighboring tone" ("suspension without preparation")
McHose:	may be on weak or strong part of beat
Ottman:	"App" — see McHose
Piston:	"app." — may be approached by repeated note (!)

6) NEIGHBORING TONE — (N)

EXAMPLE 175

Approached by skip or leap, and left by step, appearing on weak beat, or weak part of beat. Stepwise movement best in opposite direction to approach.

Goetschius:	"o" (see appoggiatura)
Hindemith:	"neighboring tone approached by skip"
McHose:	term used for auxiliary. Classed as appoggiatura
Ottman:	see McHose
Piston:	possible cambiata. Definition indefinite

7) ESCAPE TONE — (E)

EXAMPLE 176

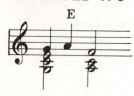

Approached by step, left by skip or leap to a chord tone. Appears on weak beat, or weak part of beat. Usually approached and left in opposite directions.

Forte:	"incomplete auxiliary note" ("suffix" type)
Hindemith:	"neighboring tone left by skip"
Ottman:	"ET"
Piston:	"éch." — "Échappée"

8) PEDAL POINT — (Pp)

EXAMPLE 177

A sustained tone, beginning and ending as part of a chord, which becomes dissonant with one or more chords of a progression. May appear anywhere, rhythmically. May appear in any voice, but usually in bass.

Forte:	over tonic or dominant
Goetschius:	"Org.-pt," "Organ-point," usually tonic, dominant, or mediant
Ottman:	"P" — "pedal"
Piston:	"ped."

While all non-chord tones are shown in the above examples in the upper voice (except the Pp), it must be understood that they may occur in any voice, barring stylistic restrictions.

Appendix B

With the information and skills acquired from a study of this text, the student should be able to arrive at an understanding of most of the music of the seventeenth and eighteenth centuries, and much of that written since, on his own.

Certain forms and techniques which are usually not possible to include in the necessarily restricted scope of the class in counterpoint are presented here for the information of the student.

ARTIFICIAL DOUBLE COUNTERPOINT

Natural double counterpoint is built around the natural process of moving two voices past each other by the octave, or intervals which add up to an octave, retaining the original harmonic structure, while the voices appear in reverse relationship. (See Chapter 13.)

Artificial double counterpoint is not a natural process, but must be arrived at by experimentation and careful planning of the original two voices. Movement of the voices across each other in any combination of intervals which do not add up to an octave belongs in this category.

1) Artificial double counterpoint *in the twelfth* is the most commonly used and the most workable. This inverting of voices will result in a change of tonality in the second version, so accidentals will need to be added, but the *size* of the interval movement will remain the same. The practicality of double counterpoint in the twelfth lies in the frequent use of the interval of a third between voices in the original counterpoint.

   a) It will be found that when the original voices are moved past each other in intervals which add up to a twelfth (or multiples of it), the original thirds will appear again as thirds, but, of course in a different key.

EXAMPLE 178

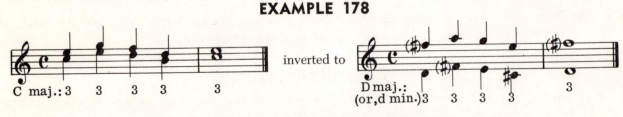

inverted to

(The lower voice has been moved upward a fourth and the upper voice downward a ninth — two intervals which add up to a twelfth.)

b) See Fugue XXIII in Book II of the *Well-Tempered Clavier*. Measures 27-29 have the original lines in tenor and soprano. Double counterpoint version appears in measures 42-44 in the soprano and alto.

2) Double counterpoint in the *eleventh* is also conceivable if the interval of the sixth is used with frequency in the original version. This interval, when its notes are moved an eleventh, will again produce a sixth.

EXAMPLE 179

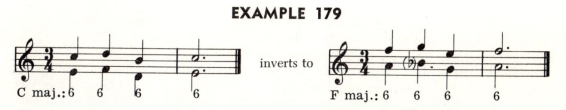

(The upper voice has been moved down a third while the lower voice has been moved up a ninth, two intervals which add up to an eleventh.)

3) Double counterpoint in the *tenth* is more difficult to produce as it requires that the first line be doubled a third below if it is the upper voice, or a third higher, if it is the lower voice, and the other line which is to be involved as double counterpoint be written against both of these lines. It is necessary that contrary motion be carefully applied to avoid parallel fifths.

EXAMPLE 180

a) The upper line is duplicated a third lower (small notes), and counterpoint in the lower line is written to these two lines (with contrary motion prevalent). The upper voice is then moved down an octave, and the lower voice up a tenth, to reverse the arrangement of the two voices.

b) The line in small notes is not intended to be used, but is a control over the notes used in the second principal line so that the upper and lower lines will work in both arrangements.

4) Other intervals of inversion are found to be used much more rarely. Most are the result of pure experimentation, and require a great deal of technical skill.

TRIPLE COUNTERPOINT

It is possible that *three* voices be written in such a manner that they may be used in other arrangements, or inversions, without disturbing their contrapuntal relationships.

1) Special care needs to be taken that each line have an individuality of its own so that the rearrangement of the voices may be noticed readily.

2) The original contrapuntal association must be as pure as possible, with predominant stepwise movement in all voices from beat to beat (except within the chord) the safest.

3) Octave inversions will be found to be the most likely. Artificial inversions will be very difficult. The only real problem will be in the range of voices, and in this type of manipulation a certain amount of crossing of voices may be unavoidable. There are six different arrangements of the original voices possible.

See Fugue XXI in Book I of the *Well-Tempered Clavier*, measures 9 through 12. These three lines are found to be rearranged several times throughout this Fugue. At times, Bach inverts individual lines in addition to rearranging the voices. Compare the above measures with measures 26 through 29. Note the freedom in the use of the subject or response versions of the thematic line interchangeably.

See also Fugue IV, Book I, measures 51 through 54 in tenor, bass, and soprano. Find further use of these three lines watching for ornamentation of part of the figure, changes of register, or use of only part of the original four measures.

THE FUGHETTA

A fughetta is, literally, a "little fugue." Generally, it will contain no more than two sections, and often, only one. The number of voices is optional, but, since the form is simple, the texture should not become too heavy.

1) The exposition follows the normal pattern found in a three-voice fugue, a four-voice fugue, or a three-voice fugue exposition with fourth statement, and is followed by a normal episode.

2) If a second section appears, it may be in the form of a rather extended coda to the single main section, or may be equal in importance to the first, beginning in a contrasting key and returning to the tonic.

3) In some cases, it may consist of no more than an exposition followed by one or two extra announcements of the subject, closing with a good cadence.

4) See the "Goldberg Variations," Variation 10.

The term, "fugato," is not synonymous with "fughetta," but refers, instead, to a section or part of a larger (predominantly homophonic) piece which is treated in an imitative (fugal) style.

THE TWO-VOICE FUGUE

This is a rare type of fugue, occurring only once in the forty-eight Fugues of the two books of the *Well-Tempered Clavier* (Fugue X, Book I). Similar patterns exist in other keyboard works of Bach but are not designated as fugues.

1) From this one example, the assumption can be drawn that the subject can be very active, to make up for the thin texture, and will be rather long with a broad range.

2) In this Fugue, the subject ends on the lowered form of the leading tone, implying dominant harmony.

3) The response is therefore at the fifth, and is a *real* response, ending on the raised fourth scale step, as part of the V/V.

4) The Fugue breaks itself into two sections at measure 20. (Note octaves for the first beat.)

5) The second part begins with a statement in the subdominant (iv), but the imitation of this, in measure 22, upper voice, is again tonic. This part is very parallel to the first part, with the last four measures serving as a codetta.

THE FIVE-VOICE FUGUE

There are only two five-voice Fugues out of the forty-eight appearing in the complete *Well-Tempered Clavier*, and these both appear in Book I (Fugues IV and XXII). This fact, along with other exceptions found in Book I and not in Book II, leads many to believe that Book I represents many of Bach's earlier experiments, and that Book II, a product of his later years, shows the results of years of discriminative experimentation.

1) A fugue containing five voices becomes, at best, very cumbersome in the matter of keyboard technique as well as in the clarity of contrapuntal devices. It is much better suited to the organ, or to an instrumental or vocal ensemble.

2) The exposition of a five-voice fugue will consist of five statements in the order of subject-response-subject-response-subject. Subject announcements will lie an octave apart, as will the response announcements.

3) The thicker texture leads to a more expanded overall range (higher first soprano and/or lower bass).

4) The order of voices in the exposition is in an adjacent pattern, from bass to soprano or from soprano to bass (Fugue IV: B-T-A-SII-SI; Fugue XXII: S-A-T-BI-BII).

5) In Fugue XXII, five-voice counterpoint is seen with the fifth entrance, and on into the first episode, while in Fugue IV, the tenor voice drops out at the fifth entrance, so that there is no real five-voice texture in the exposition.

6) After the exposition there is little five-voice counterpoint used. One voice is resting (alternating frequently), and often the texture is reduced further to three voices for long periods.

7) The subject is relatively short and of limited range. Its character is more stately and profound than many of the subjects of three- and four-voice fugues.

8) One criterion stated earlier applies here: the thicker the texture, the slower the rhythmic movement needs to be.

THE DOUBLE FUGUE

A double fugue is one in which there are *two* relatively equal subjects used, appearing simultaneously for a significant part of the fugue. This technique is more peculiar to the fugues with four or more voices, although it may be used in three-voice fugues.

The two subjects should have individual characteristics, making them strikingly independent, yet need to be conceived in flawless double counterpoint, since inversion of their relationship is characteristic of their manipulation.

The Fugue with Thematic Countersubject

In this type of double fugue, the countersubject is strong enough and important enough to be considered a subject in its own right (Subject II).

1) The countersubject recurs with the main subject throughout the exposition (except for the first statement), following the normal sequence of voices. The exposition will probably consist of one more entrance (using both subjects) than normally found.

2) Subject II continues to be associated with Subject I for the greater part of the fugue, undergoing the same manipulations.

3) Subject II may be important enough to serve as the basis of an episodic passage alone, but will not leave Subject I for long.

4) See Fugue XII, Book I. Subject II appears in measure 4 in the tenor, beginning *before* the response version of Subject I in the alto; measure 7, Subject I in bass, Subject II in alto; measure 10-12, bridge; measure 13, Subject I in soprano, Subject II in bass. The two subjects are developed together, with Subject II used as the basis of most of the episodic passages.

The Fugue with Double Subject

This type of double fugue is obvious from the beginning. The two subjects are announced together immediately.

1) The first announcement of the subjects usually utilizes adjacent voices.
2) Following the first announcement, each subject is carried through its own pattern of entrances as if it were a single subject, until each voice has stated both subjects.
3) If a four-voice fugue, the following illustration will represent one possible pattern. Other patterns will work equally well as long as the above conditions are fulfilled.

```
S —            SI(R)——SII—
A — SI————SII(R)——————————————
T — SII———————————————— SI(R)
B —            SI—————SII(R)
```

4) These same principles can be applied to three, or five voices.
5) Throughout the remaining sections of the fugue, the two subjects are manipulated together for the most part, although for short periods one or the other subject may appear alone.
6) There are no examples of this type of double fugue in the *Well-Tempered Clavier*, although a number of them may be found in Bach's organ works.

The Composite Double Fugue

This type of double fugue has the general characteristics of two fugues superimposed on one another in varying fashion.

1) Subject I may be announced and even developed for a full section by itself as in a single fugue, with Subject II joining it in a later section, and remaining as a close associate for the rest of the fugue.
2) Subject I may be announced and developed as in a single fugue. Then it may be dropped while Subject II is announced, led through an exposition of its own, and even developed. After this, both subjects will appear together for the rest of the fugue.
3) There are no examples of this type of double fugue in Book I of the *Well-Tempered Clavier*, but in Book II, Fugue IV, Subject II joins Subject I in measure 35, upper voice, with a complete statement. In Fugue XVIII, Book II, Subject II appears in measure 61 and is used alone until it combines with Subject I in measure 97 to the end.

Structural problems found in the double fugue can be more clearly stated in the media of the organ, or instrumental or vocal ensemble, where change of color, as well as texture, can help to keep the elements separated for the listener.

THE TRIPLE FUGUE

Expanding the idea of the double fugue, the triple fugue contains *three* prominent lines, individual in their characteristics, but coordinated with each other.

1) It is even more important that the three subjects be conceived, both in line and in association, as perfectly as possible.
2) The many possibilities for the utilization of three subjects can perhaps be simplified by discussing only the most common.
3) The most obvious presentation is that of having all three subjects appear together immediately, and then follow as closely as possible the normal sequence of entrances for each individual subject until each voice has stated each subject to complete the function of the exposition. An example of such an exposition for a four-voice fugue could be represented as follows:

```
S — SI————————————————SIII——SII(R)
A — SII—————SI(R)——————————SIII(R)
T — SIII————SII(R)——————SI—————————
B —          SIII(R)—————SII————SI(R)
```

a) Most examples of this type of triple fugue exposition will be found in instrumental music because of the complexity of the texture.

b) Many variants and exceptional handlings will be found.

4) Subject I and Subject II may begin together, with Subject III following immediately in one of the same voices. Strangely, one of the best examples of this type of exposition readily at hand seems to be in Sinfonia 9, in which the first and second "subjects" are announced together in the first two measures in middle and lower voices. When these two lines are moved to the two upper voices in measures 3 and 4, the third "subject" enters in the bass, immediately following the second.

A variant of this type of presentation is found in Fugue XXI, Book I, *Well-Tempered Clavier*. Subject I is stated alone in the upper voice. As it is imitated in the middle voice, the upper voice introduces Subject II (the countersubject). When the bass announces Subject I, Subject II moves to the middle voice and the upper voice announces Subject III.

5) The first complete section may be reserved for Subject I, in the manner of a single fugue. Following this, the second section of the fugue may find Subject I dropped altogether, and a complete adoption of Subject II through exposition and development, or Subject I and Subject II may be treated together, as in the double fugue. In the following section, Subject III may appear alone, or in conjunction with *either* Subject I or Subject II (*not* both). A final section will then be heard in which all three subjects appear together.

In Fugue IV, Book I, the first section is a complete exposition and episode of Subject I. In measure 35, Subject II is announced in the first soprano, while Subject I is heard in the tenor. This association of subjects prevails until measure 49, when Subject III enters in the tenor voice. All three subjects are heard equally in varying textures until measure 94, where Subject II seems to disappear. The rest of the fugue is constructed on Subjects I and III.

6) A triple fugue is exciting to think about, but it is only for the finished composer to attempt. There are too many pitfalls — artistic as well as technical — for the novice to attempt.

THE TOCCATA

The term *toccata* is generally translated to mean "touch piece" and is thought of as a keyboard piece of rather virtuosic tendencies. In this use, the word denotes a style of performance.

A toccata can also mean a sectional piece, usually in four parts, some of which may be contrapuntal in conception. It is often that these polyphonic sections be fugal in their treatment, or at least imitative in the style of a fugue, invention, or sinfonia. The other sections may be homophonic, at least one being of the aria type.

THE CANON

Supplemental to the previous presentation concerning the canon, found in Chapter 11, the following will aid in rounding out the varied treatments of this style.

Canon at Other Intervals Than the Octave

1) The canon at the fifth (fourth below), or at the fourth (fifth below) provides more possibilities for harmonic contrast than that at the octave. In order to avoid a feeling of dominant or subdominant *key*, the quality of certain intervals may need to be changed in the follower. Modulation is fine, but bitonality (each part in a different key) is impossible in this idiom.

2) Canon at the third (sixth below) or at the sixth (third below) is not too difficult if care is taken to change the quality of intervals to remain in the key.

3) Canon at the second or at the seventh perhaps presents the greatest difficulties because of the wide difference in the tonalities whose tonics are represented by the notes of these intervals and the original.

4) Canon at the unison is almost never found without a third accompanying voice to help support and define harmonic progression.

5) In canons at the unison, the second, and the third, one of the foremost problems is that of technique, since crossing of voices is almost unavoidable.

It will be found that a canon at a close time interval is more difficult to write, but will have a great deal of tension. The canonic effect may become lost if the voices follow *too* closely because the ear is not given enough of a thematic idea to grasp. Canon at wider spacings, such as after three or four measures, is much easier to hear, and form is easier to produce because it has a tendency to fall into natural phrase patterns.

Canon in Inversion (*in moto contrario*)

In this type of canon, the follower is an inverted imitation of the leader. It is best that some relationship be maintained, such as tonic being answered by the mediant or by the dominant, in order that the inverted line not stray too far afield, tonally. In the *Goldberg Variations*, both Variations 12 and 15 are canons with an inverted follower, although Bach so indicates only in 15.

EXAMPLE 181

Goldberg Variations, no. 15

(Note that G [tonic] is imitated as D [dominant] and vice versa.)

Canon in Augmentation

In this type of canon, the follower appears in note values twice as slow as the leader, so the gap between the two is always widening. It is impossible for all of the leader ever to be imitated, so a free ending is necessary.

1) It will usually begin at a close time interval.
2) Occasionally, the voices will exchange parts, or another type of canon may be resorted to.
3) It is feasible, though not common, that the follower be an inversion of the leader as well.

EXAMPLE 182

Canon in Diminution

Here, the reverse problem is found from canon in augmentation in that the follower is an imitation in notes half the value of the leader, so is soon overtaken.

1) The time interval is usually quite long.
2) When the "overtaking" takes place, the canon is either over, or the voices may shift their relationship. Another possibility is that it becomes a canon in augmentation.

EXAMPLE 183

*Note octaves appearing at point of coincidence.

The Canon in Three or More Voices

The principle of one voice leading and the others following is carried out in a three-voice canon. The same time interval and interval of imitation will occur between the two followers as between the leader and the first follower. Thus, if the first follower lies at the fifth above, and after three beats from the leader, the second follower will be at the fifth above (or fourth below) and also after three beats from the first follower.

1) If imitations are at any interval other than octave-octave, then the same requirements for changing the quality of intervals within the lines will be necessary to maintain coherence in tonality.

2) Often the first follower in a three-voice canon will work in inversion, while the second follower will again be in the original form. This is a matter for experimentation, and one serious problem arising is crossing of voices, which must be dealt with in a tasteful manner.

3) A canon in four voices requires nothing more than extension of the principles already stated for the three-voice canon.

The Double Canon

In the manner of the double fugue, this type of canon has *two* leaders heard simultaneously, with, of course, the resulting two followers. The total texture is, then, four voices. The voices are treated as in a single canon, except that they are handled as leader and follower in *pairs*.

Other canonic devices and styles, such as the round of various types, the four- and five-voice canons, and the triple canon, are not especially adaptable for the purposes of this text, which is to supply information and ideas to use as contrapuntal manipulation, as well as to help the student understand these devices when encountered.

Most of the more complicated devices are the result of "cut-and-try" experimentation, which demands perseverance and musical originality on the part of the composer, and are not subject as much to technical rules as to principles of musical taste and discrimination which, it is hoped, this text has had a small part in developing.

Bibliography

Counterpoint

BACH, J. S., *Clavier-Büchlein vor Wilhelm Friedemann Bach*, facsimile ed. New Haven, Conn.: Yale University Press, 1959.

———, *Goldberg Variations*.

———, *Two- and Three-Part Inventions*.

———, *Well-Tempered Clavier*, Books I and II.

———, *Werke*, Leipzig: Bach-Gesellschaft, 1851 – 1926.

GOETSCHIUS, PERCY, *Applied Counterpoint*, New York: G. Schirmer, Inc., 1902; reprinted 1930.

KELLY, ROBERT, *Theme and Variations*, Dubuque: Wm. C. Brown Company, 1958.

KENNAN, KENT, *Counterpoint*, Englewood Cliffs, N. J.: Prentice-Hall, Inc., 1960.

PISTON, WALTER, *Counterpoint*, New York: W. W. Norton & Company, Inc., 1947.

Theory and Analysis

FORTE, ALLEN, *Tonal Harmony in Concept and Practice*, New York: Holt, Rinehart and Winston, Inc., 1962.

GOETSCHIUS, PERCY, *Material Used in Musical Composition*, New York: G. Schirmer, Inc., 1895; 14th ed. c. 1941.

HINDEMITH, PAUL, *Traditional Harmony*, rev. ed. New York: Associated Music Publishers, Inc., 1944.

JONES, GEORGE THADDEUS, *Symbols Used in Music Analysis* (Cooperative Research Project, No. 2049), Washington, D. C.: The Catholic University of America, 1964.

KATZ, ADELE T., *Challenge to Musical Tradition*, New York: Alfred A. Knopf, 1946.

McHOSE, ALLEN IRVINE, *The Contrapuntal Harmonic Techniques of the 18th Century*, New York: F. S. Crofts & Company, 1947.

OTTMAN, ROBERT W., *Elementary Harmony; Advanced Harmony*, Englewood Cliffs, N. J.: Prentice-Hall, Inc., 1961.

PISTON, WALTER, *Harmony*, 3rd ed., New York: W. W. Norton & Company, Inc., 1962.

Special

APEL, WILLI, *Harvard Dictionary of Music*, Cambridge, Mass.: Harvard University Press, 1947.

DAVID, H. T., and MENDEL, A., eds., *The Bach Reader*, New York: W. W. Norton & Company, Inc., 1945.

Grove's Dictionary of Music and Musicians, Eric Blom, ed., 5th ed., New York: St. Martin's Press, Inc., 1954.

HINDEMITH, PAUL, *Johann Sebastian Bach, Heritage and Obligation*, New Haven, Conn.: Yale University Press, 1952.

SCHWEITZER, ALBERT, *J. S. Bach*, trans. by Ernest Newman, London: A. & C. Black, Ltd., 1923; reprinted 1945.

Index

Q

Quality, change of, 58
Quasi-imitative lines, 93

R

Range of voices:
  in 4 v texture, 141
  in 3 v texture, 94
Real response, 122
Recurrence, 16
  patterns of sequential, 17
Repeated notes:
  in first species counterpoint, 34
  in second species counterpoint, 35
  in third species counterpoint, 41
  in 3 v counterpoint, 88
Repetition, 55
  melodic and rhythmic, 16
Response:
  in a 4 v fugue, 155
  in a 3 v fugue, 122
  real, 122
  tonal, 123-125
Restatement, of subject, 157
Rests, 6
  in 4 v texture, 143
  in 3 v fugue, 137
  in 3 v texture, 91
Retrogression, 107
Rhythm:
  composite, 40
  shifted, 108
  total, 93, 148
Rhythmic:
  contrast, 18, 32
  independence, 6
  repetition, 16
Rhythmic movement, 5
  in 4 v texture, 143
  in 3 v texture, 89, 90, 93
Rhythmic placement of chords, 31

S

Scales, minor, 24
Second counterpoint:
  in sinfonias, 113
  in 3 v fugue, 131
Second species counterpoint, 35
Secondary consonances, 29
Secondary dominants, 4
  identification of, 163, 164
Sectional form, 75-77, 133
Sequence:
  in second species, 35
  in third species, 41
  melodic, 16, 53, 72
Sequential recurrence, patterns of, 17
Shifted rhythm, 108
Short sections, form in, 80, 113

Simple contrapuntal devices, 53-59
Simple meter, 7
Sinfonia (*see also,* Writing)
  counterexposition in, 113
  countermotive of, 111
  episodes of, 113
  motives and exposition of, 110
Six-four chord, 30, 67, 73, 92, 144
Size or quality, change of, 58
Skips, melodic, 11
Song form, 80
Stretto, 104
  in 4 v fugue, 159, 161
  in 3 v fugue, 136
  inversion used in, 106
  three-voice, 105
  two-voice, 106
  writing a three-voice, 135
Strong dissonance, 30
Style of eighteenth-century counter-
    point, 3
Subject:
  dominant note in, 123, 124
  modulation in, 120, 126
  of 5 v fugue, 171
  of 4 v fugue, 155
  of 3 v fugue, 119-121
  of 2 v fugue, 170
  restatement of, 157
Subordinate melodic movement, 20
Subordinate triads, 4
Subsection, 77, 133-134 (*see also*
    Sectional form)
Suspension, 9, 166
  in fourth species counterpoint, 44
Symbols:
  for analysis of non-chord tones, 10
  for thematic analysis, 73, 114, 157
Symmetry of line, 35, 41
Syncopation, 44, 87 (*see also* Tie)

T

Tempo, 144
Terminology, 162
Tessitura, 12, 69
Texture, change of, 160
Thematic considerations, 144
Third species counterpoint, 41
Third entrance in 3 v fugue, 131
Thirteenth chords, 4
Three-against-one counterpoint, 37
Three-eight time, 8, 66
Three-entrance exposition, 69
Three-part invention (*see* Sinfonia)
Three-section form:
  in fugues, 133, 159
  in inventions, 77
  in sinfonias, 113
Three-voice:
  canon, 104

counterpoint, 87
fugue, 119, 136 (*see also* Writing)
inventions (*see* Sinfonia)
stretto, 135
Tie, 6
  in fifth species counterpoint, 47
  in fourth species counterpoint, 44
  in four-voice texture, 142
  in 3 v counterpoint, 87-89
Toccata, 173
Tonal response, 123
  exceptions to, 127
  reason for, 125
Tones:
  active and altered, 5
  essential and unessential, 10
Total rhythm, 93, 148
Triads:
  frequency of use, 3
  primary, 3
  subordinate, 4
Triple counterpoint, 169
Triple fugue, 172
Triple meter, 8
Two-against-one counterpoint, 35
Two-entrance exposition, 68
Two-part invention (*see* Two-voice)
Two-section form, 77
Two-voice:
  canon, 50-52, 104
  counterpoint, 29-49
  fugue, 170
  invention, 65-84 (*see also* Writing)
  stretto, 106
  texture, harmonic implications of,
      30

U

Unessential intervals, 33
Unessential tones, 10, 25, 41
Unity and Variety:
  harmonic, 72
  in first and second species, 39
  in a canon, 51
  melodic, 16
  rhythmic, 6

V

Voices, range of:
  in 4 v texture, 141
  in 3 v texture, 94

W

Writing:
  a canon, 51
  a 4 v fugue, 161
  a sinfonia, 113
  a stretto, 135
  a 3 v fugue, 135
  a 2 v invention, 83, 84